CELEBRATING 50 GOLDEN YEARS *of the* WESLEY HISTORICAL SOCIETY- WEST MIDLANDS METHODIST HISTORY SOCIETY

1965 – 2015

CELEBRATING 50 GOLDEN YEARS
of the
WESLEY HISTORICAL SOCIETY - WEST MIDLANDS METHODIST HISTORY SOCIETY

Editors:
Donald H. Ryan
E. Dorothy Graham
Richard Ratcliffe
Diane M. Webb

Copyright © 2016 West Midlands Methodist History Society. All rights reserved. No part of this book shall be produced or transmitted in any form or by any means, electronic or mechanical, including photocopying, recording, or by any information retrieval system without written permission of the publisher.

ISBN-10: 1523280158
ISBN-13: 9781523280155

The West Midlands Methodist History Society thanks the authors of the articles used in the compilation of this book. Although every precaution has been taken in the preparation of this book, the publisher, editors and authors assume no responsibility for errors or omissions. Neither is any liability assumed for damages resulting from the use of this information contained herein.

FOREWORD

50 years of Wesley and Methodist Research

The West Midlands Branch of the Wesley Historical Society was inaugurated at a gathering of interested individuals meeting at Handsworth Methodist Ministerial Training College, Lofthouse Road, Birmingham, B20 1NN (now Handsworth Hall, Aston University). The group met on Saturday 27th March 1965. The Rev. G. Ernest Long M.A. chaired the meeting. The enthusiastic interest of those present demonstrated that there was enough support for a local branch of the Wesley Historical Society. It was agreed to call the society Wesley Historical Society – West Midlands Branch. It was further agreed that anyone who was interested in any aspects of Wesleyan/Methodist local history might join the branch by paying an annual subscription of 2/6d (12.5 pence).

The rationale of the branch was to bring together people who were interested in any aspects of Methodist history in the West Midlands. The meeting also agreed that its aim was to encourage individuals to research local Methodist history and to publish their findings in articles in the branch's bulletin or in lectures given at the branch meetings. Another aim was to get people to know the value of local church and circuit minute books, accounts, leaflets and records and the urgent need to preserve them. The scope was to include all aspects of Methodism in all its pre-1932 Methodist Union denominations as well as post-1932 Methodist churches. The meeting appointed the Rev. Dr E. Benson Perkins as the president. Dr Perkins was a greatly honoured elder statesman of British Methodism as well as a highly respected world Methodist leader. His long association with Methodism in Birmingham brought to the branch an extensive knowledge of the Methodist history in the West Midlands.

On his appointment Dr Benson Perkins spoke of the wealth of Methodist history to be found in Birmingham and the Black Country. He identified the valuable work that the branch could do for both local and Methodist history in general. He said that the branch should organise and stimulate interest in local people to research their local church and its founding members and leaders. He hoped that one day a history of Methodism in the West Midlands might be a project for the branch to pursue. The meeting elected the Rev. G. Ernest Long M.A. to be the branch chairman, Mr John A. Vickers B.A. B.D. as secretary, and Mr Stanley C. Redhead LL.B. as treasurer. With the officers appointed the meeting then proceeded to plan its next meetings. It was agreed to hold meetings twice a year in the autumn and the spring and to have a summer pilgrimage to places of Methodist interest.

The first pilgrimage was to visit Bishop Francis Asbury sites in Great Barr and Wednesbury on the 22nd May 1965. The autumn meeting was arranged to be held on Saturday 25th September at Handsworth College. The meeting agreed to publish the formation of the branch widely and to encourage as many people as possible to join. There were 16 founding members of the branch and, within a year, 45 members and 17 libraries were subscribing.

A little over a year after the inaugural meeting, the society took on the project to arrange a conference exhibition to coincide with the Methodist Conference meeting in Wolverhampton. The exhibition consisted of 114 exhibits ranging from original letters from John Wesley, Charles Wesley and John Fletcher, vicar of Madeley, to John Wesley's *Field Bible 1653* with notes in his handwriting, and his preaching bands. The exhibition included several busts, figures and plaques of John Wesley. Also included in the exhibition was the wooden dessert service (c.1550-1600), which was a wedding gift to Rev. Dr Adam Clarke from John Wesley. There were several important artefacts relating to early Methodism in Staffordshire, Wolverhampton, Shropshire, and the Black Country. The exhibition, entitled '**Methodism Past And Present**' was held in the art gallery on Lichfield Street, Wolverhampton, from 27th June to 16th July 1966.

The next major project the society undertook was to organise and mount an exhibition that was opened on 30th June 1969 at the Birmingham Museum and Art Gallery to celebrate the 75th anniversary of the founding of the Wesley Historical Society, the parent body of the West Midlands Wesley Historical Society. The exhibition coincided with the Methodist conference meeting in the city. The main organiser of the exhibition was a member of the Wesley Historical Society – West Midlands, Miss Doreen Pooler M.B.E. Items of special interest included relics from Madeley Parish Church and the Wednesbury riots. Artefacts from the National Children's Home were included to celebrate their centenary along with memorabilia of the first Wesleyan conference held in Birmingham in 1836.

In 1976, a Wesley exhibition of 109 items was mounted by Rev. Donald H. Ryan in the Wolverhampton Art Gallery from 17th April to 1st May. The exhibition was organised to be an added value extra feature to the professional production of *Ride! Ride!* (the Wesley musical: book and lyrics by Alan Thornhill, music by Penelope Thwaites), which was playing at Wolverhampton Grand Theatre during its national UK tour before opening at the Westminster Theatre, London, in May.

From the start of the WHS West Midlands there have been outstanding lectures delivered twice a year by excellent Methodist historians on local, national and international subjects. The society has produced occasional publications. No.1 publication, *The Methodist New Connexion in Dawley and Madeley* (Barrie Trinder B.A. 1967, Adult Education tutor Salop County Council), No.2 publication, *The Origins of Primitive Methodism in the West Midlands 1800-1850* (a transcript of the lecture delivered on October 18th 1969 at Quinton Methodist Church by Rev. Dr J. T. Wilkinson M.A., transcript made by D. L. Eades, editor of the branch), No.3 publication, *Silver Jubilee Miscellany 1965-1990*.

We honour the faithful officers who have, with vision and enthusiasm, kept the society focused and committed to the original principles laid down 50 years ago.

President
Rev. Dr. E. Benson Perkins M.A. 1965-1974

Joint Presidents
Rev. C. Hughes Smith M.A. 1976-1986
Rev. Nigel Gilson D.F.C. M.A. 1976-1988
Rev. Donald M. Eadie 1988-1995
Rev. Dr T. John Sampson 1989-1999
Rev. Christina Le Moignan M.A. 1996-2003

Rev. Peter F. Curry B.A. 2000-2005
Rev. William H. Anderson B.A. 2001-2012
Rev. John D. Howard M.A. M.Min. B.Sc. 2006-2016
Rev. Ian Howarth M.A. 2013-

Chairman
Rev. G. Ernest Long M.A. 1965-1967
Rev. Geoffrey Robson M.A. 1968-1977
Rev. Donald G. Knighton M.A. 1979-1983
Rev. W. Stanley Rose B.D. 1984-1986
Rev. Dr. David F. Clarke 1988-1993
Rev. Ian Haile B.Met. 1993-1998
Rev. Donald H. Ryan M.Th. 1999-

Deputy Chairman
Rev. Derick Chambers B.A. 2013-2015

Secretary
Mr John A. Vickers B.A. B.D. 1965
Dr E. Dorothy Graham B.A. B.D. 1966-2010

Organising Secretary
Mrs Diane Webb 2011-

Minutes Secretary
Mr Richard Ratcliffe F.S.G. 2011-

Treasurer
Mr Stanley C. Redhead LL.B. 1965-1988
Mr Leslie E. Collins B.Sc. 1989-1992
Mr John S. Randerson 1993-2014

Mr John Bevins 2015-

Editor
Mr John A. Vickers B.A. B.D. 1966-1967
Mr David L. Eades J.P. M.Ed. 1968-1974
(Acting) Rev. & Mrs Geoffrey Robson 1975-1977
Mr J. J. Rowley M.A. 1977
Rev. Donald H. Ryan 1978-1981
Mr Stanley C. Redhead LL.B. 1981-1988
Mr Paul Bolitho M.A. A.L.A. 1989-

Archivist
Mr E. Lissimore B.Sc. 1967
Mr Geoffrey Beard 1968-1972
Mr David L. Eades J.P. M.Ed. 1973-1976
Mr Thomas K. Skinner I.S.M. 1978-2003
Mrs Sheila Himsworth B.A. 2004-

Publicity Officer
Mrs Diane Webb 2007-

Elected Member
Miss D. M. Pooler M.B.E 1965-1971
Mr G. M. Brain 1966-1971
Mr K. E. Witts 1966-1967
Mr Thomas K. Skinner 1968-1977
Rev. Donald H Ryan 1972-1977
Rev. J. Munsey Turner M.A. 1973-1980
Mrs Millie Skinner 1978-2012
Mr G. Elliott 1978-1983
Rev. Gordon Wakefield M.A. M.Lit 1981-1983

Mrs M. Hulton M.A. 1984-1987
Mr Paul Bolitho M.A. A.L.A. 1987-1988
Mr D. L. Robinson 1988-1991
Mr John S. Randerson 1989-1992
Rev. Colin C. Short B.Sc, B.D 1992-2000
Mr Leslie E. Collins 1993-2002
Mrs Diane Webb 2001-2006
Mr Richard Ratcliffe F.S.G. 2007-2010
Dr E. Dorothy Graham 2011-
Mr John Bevins 2011-2014

When the Wesley Historical Society pioneered the opening of area branches of the society its primary aim was to encourage the research and study of Methodism in the area where the branch was located.

The West Midlands Wesley Historical Society in 2011 voted to change its name. The original name had historic roots in Wesleyan Methodism but, after careful discussion, it was agreed to change the name to the West Midlands Methodist History Society. The members wished to reflect the broadening of the scope of study and interest to all branches of Methodism in the West Midlands.

Donald H. Ryan

CONTENTS

Quinton Methodist Church	1
Bourne College	9
Aston Villa Methodist Church	20
Reflections From An Ordination At Handsworth	27
Blackheath And Halesowen Methodism	33
Blackwood Methodist Church 50th Anniversary	41
Bristol Road And Northfield Methodist Churches	50
Four Oaks Methodist Church	59
A Small Place In Leyfields	65
Springdale Methodist Church	70
Engelberg Methodist Home 50th Anniversary	81
Observing Methodist Worship Worcester 1940 & 1973	91
Bishop Francis Asbury	103
Bertie Bissell	109
Sons Of Franklyn G. Smith	118
Methodist Million	124
Wesley Deaconess Convocation, Birmingham	130
Archives And Heritage	140

CONTRIBUTORS

Dr Michael Hall, M.A. F.C.P. Birmingham West and Oldbury Circuit Archivist; local preacher for over 50 years. In 2013, he was awarded a British Association for Local History Personal Achievement Award.

E. Dorothy Graham B.A. B.D. Ph.D. From a family with a strong preaching tradition, she has been a local preacher for 61 years. Brought up in Warwickshire, educated there and at the universities of Leeds and Birmingham. Taught in Scotland, Yorkshire and Birmingham. Secretary of the West Midlands WHS (1966-2010); General Secretary of the WHS (1980-2006); and Connexional Archives Liaison Officer (1989-2001). Publications: various articles on local history, Primitive Methodist women preachers, and the Wesley Deaconesses Order. Lives in Birmingham.

Rev. Lionel E. Osborn. President of the Methodist Conference 2011; Former Chair of the Newcastle upon Tyne Methodist District.

Rev. Donald H. Ryan M.Th. Former Chair of the North Wales Methodist District; Former Chair of the Methodist Connexional Local Archives and Oral History Committee; Registrar, Administrator and Webmaster of Wesley Historical Society; Chair of the West Midlands Methodist History Society. Publications: articles in the Wesley Historical Society

Proceedings, also in the Bulletins of The West Midlands Methodist History Society, Shropshire Wesley Historical Society, The Lancashire Wesley Historical Society and entries in the Dictionary of Methodism in Britain and Ireland.

David L. Eades J.P. M.Ed. Editor of the West Midlands Methodist History Society 1968-1974 and Archivist 1973- 1976. Previously Birmingham Methodist District Archivist, and Circuit Archivist of the Halesowen Methodist Circuit. Currently Joint Circuit Archivist of the Blackheath and Halesowen Methodist Circuit. Former Circuit Steward and Local Preachers' Secretary as well as other church offices. A local preacher for 52 years.

John Harden. Joint Church Secretary, Blackwood Methodist Church.

Jim Hart. Council Secretary, Four Oaks Methodist Church. Member of the Birmingham District Council.

Dr. P. W. Rickwood. Founder member and Church Steward, St Andrew's Methodist Church, Tamworth.

Clive D. Field O.B.E. D.Litt. Honorary Research Fellow in the School of History and Cultures, University of Birmingham and a former Director of Scholarship and Collections at The British Library. He has been bibliography editor of the Wesley Historical Society for 42 years and a member of the West Midlands Methodist History Society since 1976.

Richard Ratcliffe F.S.G. Retired Head Teacher, former Archives Liaison Officer for the Federation of Family History

Societies; President of the Lincolnshire Family History Society (1990-2010); President of the Birmingham & Midlands Society of Genealogy & Heraldry (2002–2012); Part-time Archivist, Westminster Methodist Central Hall, London (2002–2009); responsible for getting the Wesleyan Methodist Historic Roll microfilmed, indexed and refurbished. Currently transcribing the first six volumes of the Historic Roll.

Diane Webb. Birmingham Methodist District Archivist, West Midlands Methodist History Society; Meetings/Organising Secretary.

Kath Collman. Birmingham Circuit Archivist Team.

Memoirs of Thomas Skinner (1913-2002) supplied by his family. Elmdon Circuit Archivist and Wesley Historical Society; West Midlands Branch Archivist until his death in 2002.

QUINTON METHODISM IN THE BIRMINGHAM (WEST) & OLDBURY CIRCUIT

On February 3rd 1968, with a congregation filling the premises, Methodism opened its new Quinton church. This event provided a journalistic field day, not rejoicing in denominational success but revelling in electronic failure. "It was Miss Partridge's big day: she had been a member of Quinton Methodist Church since she was a child 86 years ago, and yesterday she was to open the new church. She cut the tape and sat down with 700 people for Rev. Brian S. O'Gorman's sermon. But all Miss Partridge and the startled congregation heard were BBC Radio Two's the Mark Roman Pop Show. Church officials dashed to turn down the public address system, Rev. O'Gorman started to shout, little Miss Partridge and the congregation strained to hear, but the disc jockey's non-stop patter continued and the hit parade played on."[1]

[1] *The Sunday Mercury* 04.02.1968
[2] Quinton Methodist Church Trustees' Meeting Minutes 05.12.1963

That the congregation seated within the church was unaware of the problems in ancillary rooms would obviously have spoiled a good story!

The new church was needed when the previous site was compulsorily purchased for the building of the M5. Trustee reaction to the order was pragmatic: "The implications were given careful consideration and no valid objections anticipated provided a suitable site and adequate compensation were forthcoming."[2]

The building being replaced, opened by Primitive Methodists in nearby College Road in 1888 (itself a replacement of an earlier chapel), was in 1935 the setting for a merger with Quinton's Wesleyans, whose minister reported the success of the venture. "When the union took place some of our people joined College Road choir. At their first rehearsal, the choirmaster asked newcomers to seat themselves and then the rest of the choir would take their places. More than once have I quoted Quinton as the way in which union is achieved."[3] Hagley Road Wesleyan Chapel, opened in 1878 on the Turnpike Road, replaced Quinton's first preaching house, built on the estate of local benefactor, Ambrose Foley, and remaining private property

---

[2] Quinton Methodist Church Trustees' Meeting Minutes 05.12.1963
[3] Letter from Rev. Norman Upright 08.07.1980

bequeathed in Foley's will 'to Richard Longmore and Thomas Floyd, preachers of the Gospel'.[4]

Longmore and Floyd preached alternately in Foley's chapel, the former until his death and the latter until 1846 when the preachers' meeting enquired 'into case of Quinton to ascertain if Bro Floyd be under the necessity of preaching in that chapel every fortnight'.[5]

Subsequently, representatives met Floyd to ascertain 'if he will sign an agreement (for) a lease on the chapel free from all encumbrance'.[6] The outcome, reported in an early circuit history, was that Floyd 'surrendered for a money consideration the bequest to which he had legal claim'.[7]

Quinton Methodism resulted from Foley hearing John Wesley preach and deciding that villagers should have a similar experience. He built in his garden a hermit house where agricultural labourers and nailers could meet to hear the Scriptures and Wesley's sermons. In 1778, Foley wrote inviting Wesley to visit Quinton: "If you have an hour or two to spare, my house which is a good one, and my heart, which is a bad one, are both open to you . .

---

[4] Ambrose Foley *Last Will and Testament* 09.12.1826 Lee Crowder papers 383-385 Library of Birmingham
[5] Birmingham Local Preachers' Meeting Minutes 09.01.1846
[6] Birmingham Local Preachers' Meeting Minutes 19.06.1846
[7] Barr, David, "Village Methodism: How Methodism came to Quinton" in *Christian Miscellany* (December 1890)

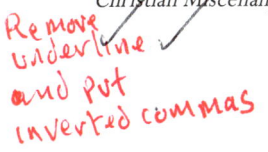

."[8] Wesley did have an hour or two to spare but not for three years, visiting Quinton in March 1781 with further visits following.[9] The work obviously prospered and on Easter Sunday 1785 Wesley recorded in his *Journal*, "Notice had been given of my preaching at Quinton. As the house would not hold the people, I was constrained, cold as it was, to preach abroad."[10] By Wesley's return the following year, Foley's preaching house had opened.

Some 40 years after Wesley's visit, William Stringer, a Darlaston local preacher, introduced Primitive Methodism to Quinton when Mr Deeley of Tinker's Farm offered his house for worship. In 1827, the 'Prims' removed to Samuel Chatwin's Monckton Farm and 'a stall in the barn, which was cleaned out on Saturday night (where) our Sunday-school children were huddled on Sunday mornings, while the preaching service was conducted in the barn'.[11] Here worship continued until 1840 when Bethesda Chapel opened so close to Foley's preaching house that the singing in one chapel could be heard in the other! Early progress amongst Quinton's Primitive Methodists was fragile. "Our preachers were much persecuted; they were pelted with rotten eggs; the windows of their place of worship were broken and their services disturbed by bands of music."[12] In reaction, Darlaston Circuit resolved that 'the Society at Quinton print handbills and 2 guineas reward be offered to any person

---

[8] Ambrose Foley to John Wesley 18.03.1778 in Hackwood, F.W., *Oldbury and Round About* (1915)
[9] See Wesley's *Journal* 24.03.1781; 1784; 26.03.1785; 21.03.1786; 1788;19.03.1790
[10] Wesley, John, *Journal* (edited by Nehemiah Curnock) 1938 - 26.03.1785
[11] McKechnie, Colin, *The Life of Hugh Bourne* (1892)
[12] Flesher, John (ed) *Primitive Methodist Magazine* (1850)

who shall impeach on the persons who have persecuted that society'.[13] Later, landmarks were encouraged, when in 1912 Quinton's 'Prims' enjoyed the generosity of manufacturer Edwin Danks who, at the request of his coachman, the society's steward, built a house for the minister in the village. Like its Wesleyans, Quinton's Primitive Methodists were visited by the founding fathers: William Clowes in 1845 and Hugh Bourne frequently from 1836, for which he received local recognition when in 1882, Bourne College, a school for the sons of Primitive Methodists, opened in the village.[14]

Bourne College challenged Quinton parochialism. During its 47 year life it was attended by 39 local boys and 1,159 from locations as distant as Fernando Po from where Rev. Napoleon Barleycorn sent his sons to be educated. Local pulpits benefited. "The services of the Governor and masters are much desired in the chapels in the neighbourhood . . . Some seem to think that they can get served as easily as though it were a college for the training of ministers. However talent is not the first thing required for these chapels. If the youth has the love of God in his heart, his efforts are blessed."[15] Two college men (both of whom are buried in Quinton Old Cemetery) stand out in local Methodist history: Headmaster T. J. S. Hooson, for over 40 years Treasurer, Circuit Secretary and local preacher, and Rev. George Middleton, College Governor, Circuit Steward and Parish Council Chairman.

---

[13] Darlaston Primitive Methodist Circuit Meeting Minutes 05.04.1827
[14] Bourne College began life in 1876 in the redundant St Chad's Grammar School in Summer Hill, Birmingham
[15] Middleton, George (ed) *Bourne College Chronicle* I 1887-1888

Following WW1, increased provision of state secondary education obviated the need for minor public schools and Bourne College closed in 1928. The school's influence upon Quinton's Primitive Methodism should never be underestimated, not least for the presence of its staff and students at worship, which necessitated the building of College Road Chapel to replace Bethesda. Thus, when the new Quinton Methodist Church opened in February 1968, it was the eighth dedicated Methodist building in Quinton within a radius of 200 yards. In addition to all the usual weekday Methodist pursuits, and aided by its arrival in the village ahead of any Anglican presence,[16] Quinton Methodism has always exercised a vital community role. Today it is expressed in the diverse groups using the premises for activities ranging from quilting to Spanish, line dancing to photography and keep fit to art. A luncheon club caters for the community as well as the congregation. Since 1970, 45 annual projects have supported charities beyond the Methodist family both at home and abroad. £200,000 has been raised, in addition to normal weekly giving and other special events like the book sale, which raised £2,500 supporting the work of Birmingham University's Theology Department, undertaken in recognition of the stationing of Rev. Prof Frances Young in the circuit. Members of the local community are welcomed by such church-based activities as arts, flower and Christmas festivals, holiday clubs and Passover meals. In all this, the church's reason for being here – to share the love of God and to join together in worship – is paramount. That message reached far beyond Quinton when the congregation led Radio Four's morning service and Sunday Half

---

[16] Quinton Parish Church was consecrated in September 1840

Hour.[17] In 2015, wider Methodism is indebted to all that Ambrose Foley started here, as Rev. Kenneth G. Howcroft, President of Conference (2014-2015) candidated from Quinton Methodist Church.

John Wesley's *Journal* for March 1781 notes: "I was invited to preach at Quinton, five miles from Birmingham. I preached there at noon, in the open air, to a serious and attentive congregation. Some of them appeared to be very deeply affected. Who knows but it may continue?"[18] Continue it has, and for that we give thanks to God.

Dr Michael Hall

---

[17] On 14.04.1985 and 28.12.1986 respectively
[18] Wesley, John, *Journal* (edited by Nehemiah Curnock) 1938 - 24.03.1781;

Date	Wesleyan Chapel	Wesleyan Circuit	Primitive Methodist Chapel	Primitive Methodist Circuit
c1775	Foley's 'Hermit House'			
1786	Foley's Preaching House			
c1818			Deeley's Farm Barn	
1827			Chatwin's Farm Barn	Darlaston
1828				Birmingham East
1838		Birmingham West		
1840			Bethesda	
1864		Cherry Street		
1867				Old Hill
1871		Islington		
1876	Hagley Road			
1888			College Road	Blackheath & Quinton
1901				Quinton / Birmingham Sixth / Quinton & Bourne College
	Methodist Chapel		**Methodist Circuit**	
1935	College Road		Birmingham (Quinton)	
1963			Islington-Quinton	
1968	Quinton			
1980			Birmingham (West)	
1993			Birmingham (West) & Oldbury	

BOURNE COLLEGE, QUINTON, BIRMINGHAM (1876-1928)

In July 1875, the Rev. George Middleton, Superintendent Minister of Summer Hill Primitive Methodist Society, and others bought a house on Summer Hill, previously occupied by St Chad's Roman Catholic Grammar School. They intended to establish 'a School for the Midlands . . .' George Middleton became both Secretary and Governor and Mr R. G. Heys B.A., Headmaster. The first students entered the college in January 1876.[19] The May 1877 *Primitive Methodist Magazine* reported that "Bourne College, Birmingham, is rapidly taking up a good position, and is likely to develop into a useful and effective middle class educational institution . . . There is some talk about securing land and erecting more commodious premises."[20]

An analysis of the first intake reveals that 25 pupils, ranging in age from 8-17, were registered. Some were sons of Primitive Methodist itinerants and others came from local families. The length of stay varied from 5 to 35 months. They were put into three classes, chiefly by age, and details about their knowledge on entry recorded.[21]

---

[19] *Bourne College Chronicle 5* (hereafter *BCC*) (1895-1901) pp. 161ff; Kendall, H.B., *The Origins and History of the Primitive Methodist Church* 2 vols. (n.d. ?1904) vol.2 p.525
[20] *Primitive Methodist Magazine* (hereafter *PMM*) (1877) p.313
[21] MSS Bourne College Entry Book I (1876-92)

From 1878, the *Primitive Methodist* minutes contain the Annual Report and Accounts, which deal mainly with the students' educational prowess, though occasionally other information is given. For example, the second year report states that the college was full, averaging 50 students, 12% of whom were ministers' sons and that the headmaster, Mr Heys, taught science with the boys being very interested in physiology. There were French, Greek and Latin classes and 'a native for the German language' visited the school weekly. The mathematical curriculum included 'algebraic and geometrical classes', whilst the religious side was encouraging as some boys were now members and also on the preachers' plan.[22]

In 1879, the trustees formed a limited liability company and purchased land at Quinton for £3,210 from Mr James Nott, one of the trustees.[23] The first building plans were rejected as too costly, but a further tender, guaranteeing that 'the cost would not be more than £6,700 including steam engine, heating apparatus, water tanks, gas-fittings, outbuildings, and everything else necessary', was accepted. Following the purchase of the 19 acre estate, many improvements were made to the grounds. Five acres in front of the college were designated for the playground, space on the north side as gardens for the boys and nearly two acres became kitchen gardens, hopefully to produce enough vegetables for the college.[24]

The intention was to provide a middle-class education for the sons of Primitive Methodist ministers and laymen, or other Nonconformist or Methodist bodies with 'a curriculum . . .

---

[22] *PMMins* (1878) pp.91-4
[23] *PMMins* (1879) pp.84-9
[24] *PMMins* (1883) pp.82-84; *BCC 5* (1895-1901) pp. 163-64

embracing all commercial and classical subjects (including mathematical and languages) for professions, University Examination and matriculation; taking care also to promote their spiritual interests and their instruction in the principles of our Christian faith'.[25]

Rather optimistically, it was hoped that building would begin in 1881 and the college be ready for use by February.[26] However, it was not until after the 1882 Midsummer break that the college moved to Quinton with the official opening ceremony, held in pouring rain, taking place on 24th October 1882. A lengthy article in a local magazine gives an independent account of the college, remarking that its purpose was to extend educational opportunities and describing its situation, the building and its facilities.[27]

21 students moved to Quinton from Summer Hill and another 18 enrolled during the first year.[28] T. J. S. Hooson, B.A., aged nearly 21, was appointed as its one and only Headmaster. Thomas James Stewart Hooson, son of Stewart Hooson, a Primitive Methodist minister, was born on 16th February 1862 and educated at both Elmfield and Bourne Colleges. The Entry Book records his entry and progress and the 1899 *Bourne College Chronicle* reads "Mr Hooson entered . . . early in 1878, as a student. . . Ere the close of 1878 he had been elected . . . to a junior post on the staff. His work ever since has stamped him as a born teacher."[29] Hooson completed his London

---

[25] *PMM* (1879) pp. 762-63
[26] *PMMins (1881) pp. 96-98*
[27] *Birmingham Places and Faces* 2nd November 1891
[28] *BCC 5* (1895-1901) pp.241-3; MSS - Bourne College Entry Book I pp.9f
[29] *BCC 5* (1895-1901) pp.241-3

University B.A. in 1884 and then took an Intermediate B.Sc. at Mason College, later Birmingham University, so he was well qualified to be the headmaster.

In 1887/8 the Board decided to issue a magazine, *Chronicle*, and the ones that have survived provide many interesting details and sidelights on the college activities. Quinton Primitive Methodist chapel proved too small when its congregations were swelled by Bourne College staff and boys, so in 1883 it was decided to sell the old chapel and start a New Chapel Building Fund. The college helped with fund raising, especially through musical concerts. Foundation stones were laid on June 25th 1888, and it opened on 18th November when the Governor conducted some of the services.[30] Apparently, over the years the services of the masters and indeed some of the boys were required to fill preaching appointments locally as Hooson commented: "The services of the Governor and Masters are much desired at the chapels in the neighbourhood, belonging to all denominations . . . . I often find officials . . . going to the college a few hours before the service, to get a supply in cases of unexpected disappointment. Some seem to think that they can get served as easily as though it were a college for the training of ministers. However, talent is not the first thing that is required in these chapels. If the youth or young man has the love of God in his heart, he can tell of Jesus and his power to save and his efforts are blessed."[31]

---

[30] College Road PM Church Trustees Minutes 1882-1927 (December 1883); *BCC* 1(1887-8) pp.155-6; 5 (1895-1901) p.34

[31] *BCC* 1 (1887-8) p.87

The college prospered and the Summer Hill debt was cleared by 1892 with a dividend paid to shareholders.[32] In 1889 and 1890, enjoyable concerts were held, the proceeds providing two turf tennis courts, tennis equipment and re-laying half the cricket pitch.[33] The encouraging 1893 report has some items of special interest, particularly that the Conference Scholarship had been awarded to J. H. Banks, son of a prominent Willenhall Baptist. Perhaps this shows Bourne College's popularity and open-minded attitude in keeping faith with its aims of providing a first class education for Nonconformist as well as Primitive Methodist boys. Rather intriguingly, the accounts record that a 'Farm Account Deficiency, arose through death of a Milch Cow - £5.12s 6d'.[34]

From the beginning the college had had overseas students and in 1894 it is noted that "Rowland E. Barleycorn of Fernando Po . . . passed in every subject . . ."[35] Rowland was the son of the Rev. William Napoleon Barleycorn, a native of Fernando Po and an early convert to Primitive Methodism. Mr Barleycorn had visited the college in September 1887, when he sang to the boys 'in Boobee, his native language'. It was probably this visit that prompted him to send his sons to Bourne. The *Chronicle* has several articles from the Rev. R. W. Burnett, a missionary in Fernando Po whose sons attended the college. On one visit he gave a talk 'on the habits of the natives and their peculiarities' bringing 'with him . . . a couple of African parrots'.[36] No doubt

---

[32] *PMMins.* (1889)p.137; (1890)p.133; (1891) p.147; (1892) pp. 156-58
[33] *BCC, 2* (1888-9) pp.156-8, 165; *3* (1889-90) pp.37-8, 169-70
[34] *PMMins* (1893)pp.159-161; *BCC 5* (1895-1901) p. 136
[35] *PMMins* (1894) pp.154-7; cf. BCC 5 (1895-1901) pp.29, 70
[36] *BCC 1* (1887-8) p.187

such visits heightened the college's interest in the Connexion's work in Africa, so that £6 was collected at the first missionary meeting. The *Chronicle* notes that, chiefly due to pressure from the college, Birmingham Corporation extended its gas main 2½ miles to provide it with gas and, that after some initial local suspicion, street lamps had been erected in Quinton. Later articles report various gifts including a 'new American Organ' and that the Governor and Headmaster had been elected to the Parish Council as 'progressive Candidates'.[37] When an Extension Scheme provided more accommodation and better facilities, the curriculum was revised 'to adapt it to modern ideas and requirements' and more staff engaged.[38]

Bourne College Calendar details school events and achievements but is also a prospectus, listing the staff and the subjects taught and describing the premises and grounds, including the information that 'Cows are kept'. The college year was divided into three equal terms, commencing in mid-January, near the end of April, and mid-September. The boys had two weeks vacation at Easter, seven weeks in the summer and four weeks at Christmas. Reports were sent to parents or guardians three times a year.[39]

The curriculum indicates an all round education, showing that the boys should reach a very satisfactory academic standard, although Hooson protested that he felt the College of Preceptors' 1888 Christmas examination was expecting rather a lot when it asked for a full account of 'The Inter-colonial Railway System of the Dominion of Canada' or of the 'Egyptian Dynasties' and the

---

[37] *BCC* 5 (1895-1901) pp.244, 262, 282-3
[38] *PMMins* (1899) pp.154-7
[39] *Bourne College Calendar* 1899 pp.8-10

'Parliaments of Bats'.[40] However, it was not all work and no play because the college prided itself that 'in the matter of Homeliness, Bourne College does its utmost to make the students happy without weakening its discipline. Believing also that proper physical culture is a great auxiliary to the brain, various popular games are encouraged out of school hours'.[41] Hooson himself was a proficient footballer, tennis player, and especially a cricketer. His modern attitude to education and his belief that it should cater for the whole person is shown when Swedish Drill (taught by) 'Miss A. Ryding and Miss Smith (from the Anstey Physical Training Centre' were members of staff in 1909-1910. It seems that Hooson was keeping faith with the Primitive Methodist ethos of using the best possible means to hand to fulfil their purpose. Visits were made to exhibitions and displays in Bingley Hall, Birmingham, to recitals in Halesowen, to the Clent Hills, to Edwin Danks' Boiler Works and to see visiting dignitaries, such as the Prime Minister, Mr Gladstone, and the Shah of Persia.[42]

Extra-curricular activities included the popular Social Circle, which had a variety of speakers and debates on topical subjects. It is clear the boys were given the chance to become familiar with life in the outside world and to practise the art of public speaking that would stand many of them in good stead in pulpits and secular professions. In 1908, a patrol of Boy Scouts was started

---

[40] *BCC 2* (1888-9) p.85
[41] *Bourne College Calendar* 1897 p.23
[42] *Bourne College Calendar* 1909 p.5 *BCC 5* (1898-1901) pp. 227-28, 132; *BCC 7 (1908-1913) (1911) pp.20-1, pp.(1909) pp.80-84; BCC 2 (1888-1889) pp.25,45,46,206*

and during the 1910 General Election, a mock election was held.[43]

Tax increases and higher fuel prices caused a drop in revenue in 1901, while the Government's proposals on secondary education and its possible effect on 'the popularly-controlled education' caused concern. For the first time in 20 years the college reported a deficit in 1906 and blamed trade depression and the establishment of State Schools for causing some parents to withdraw their children. A further deficit in 1907, due to heating problems and a serious loss in farm stock, had to be met from the Reserve Fund, but pupil numbers were up so the outlook seemed rather better.[44] The Rev. George Middleton F.G.S. died on November 3rd 1907, aged 77. Officially he had been Governor, Secretary, Chaplain and unofficially Bursar, Caretaker-in-chief, handyman and general odd job man as well as being active in the local Primitive Methodist Church and circuit, preaching frequently. The Directors appointed the Headmaster as Governor and the local Primitive Methodist minister became Chaplain.

Over the next few years more students entered and finances improved. Also the growth of Birmingham, including 'the incorporation of Quinton with Birmingham', was likely to enhance the estate's value and local house building might mean more boys attending the college, while 'a system of Motor Buses (running) from New Street to Quinton every hour' had improved access.[45]

---

[43] *BCC 7* (1908-13) pp.60, 91-3
[44] *PMMins* (1906) pp.181 (1907) pp.190-3-37
[45] *PMMins* (1911) pp.231-37; cf *BCC 7* (1908-13) p.75; *PMMins* (1913) p.230; (1914) p.224

During WW1 around 300 old boys served in the forces with many receiving bravery awards. In 1916, the college insurances were increased 'to cover all aircraft risks'.[46] The Old Boys decided to found an open scholarship and also fund a memorial tablet to those who 'gave their lives for their country'. This tablet, containing 30 names, was unveiled at the Annual Prize Giving in July 1921.[47] When the college closed in 1928, it was taken to College Road Primitive Methodist Chapel, but apparently destroyed when that chapel was demolished in 1967/8.

In 1920 the college, for the first time in its history, had over 100 boys on the register and consequently an improved financial position, meaning that the outlook was promising.[48] In spite of 'industrial disputes and trade depression', numbers increased in 1927, but the financial deficiency was still very large and after that, matters took a downward turn.[49] By May 1928 it was obvious that this state of affairs could not continue so it was decided 'to raise a fund to put matters on a better footing (and) to work . . . to clear off the floating liabilities; to provide for necessary renovations and improvements and to establish annual Scholarships and prizes'.[50] A Jubilee Celebration, held on Whit Tuesday 1928, included a cricket match between the Old Boys and the college, which the Old Boys won by 50 runs. The

---

[46] *PMMins* (1915) p.227; (1917) p.189; *BCC 8* and *9* (1913-21); (1916) p.1; (1919) pp.17,26-32; *PMMins* (1916) p.178
[47] *PMMins* (1919) p.196; (1920) p.191; (1921) p.191; cf. *BCC 8* and *9* (1920) pp.1-2; *BCC 10* (1922-28), (1921) p.1; cf. picture facing p.12; *PMMins* (1922) p.195
[48] *PMMins* (1920) p. 191;(1922) p.195; (1923) p.192; (1924) p.201
[49] *PMMins* (1927) pp.217-18
[50] *PMMins* (1928) pp.213-16

Chairman of the Board commended the Jubilee Fund, but unfortunately just under £500 out of the appeal for £5,000 was raised.[51] In spite of the precarious financial position, 9 boys were accepted in September 1928. Of the 54 students there, almost 76% were local so it is quite conceivable that some, if not all, were day boys.[52] It seems the college finally closed its doors at the end of that autumn term, but the Primitive Methodist minutes make no reference to it. It is possible that the prospect of Methodist Union may also have contributed to the fall in numbers and the consequent financial problems, which brought about the college's demise. The contents were auctioned on March 13th and 14th 1929 and its scholarships transferred to Elmfield. The buildings were sold to the Birmingham Board of Guardians for £9,675 and in 1930, having been refurbished and renamed Quinton Hall, it re-opened as a Poor Law Convalescent Home for Aged Men.[53] It was closed and demolished in 1979 and a housing estate built on the site.

At the Old Boys' Dinner on March 7th 1930, Mr Hooson was presented with a cheque for £450 to mark his 50 years association with the college.[54] He died in February 1931 and, following the funeral service at College Road Primitive Methodist Church on 24th February, was interned at Quinton Old Cemetery.[55] Thomas James Stewart Hooson never married. It would be true to say that Bourne College was not only his life, but also his family.

[51] *BCC 10* (1928) pp.5-6
[52] MSS - Day Book 2 (1893-1928)
[53] *The Birmingham Post,* Friday 22 March 1929
[54] *The Birmingham Mail,* Friday 7 March 1930; *The Evening Dispatch,* Friday 7 March 1930
[55] *The Birmingham Gazette,* Wednesday 25 February 1931; *The County Express,* Saturday 28 February 1931

In its short history of just over 50 years Bourne College provided, as its academic and musical record shows, a very good all round education. It had been a brave exciting venture but had served its purpose by 1928.

E. Dorothy Graham

NOTE: A full account of Bourne College is to be found on the website http://www.primitivemethodistwomen.org

ASTON VILLA METHODIST CHURCH. THE STORY OF 100 YEARS 1850-1950

Extracts from the Aston Villa Methodist Church Centenary Handbook

The first Methodist chapel to be built in Birmingham was at Cherry Street in July 1782, quickly followed by those in Bradford Street in 1786 and Belmont Row in 1789. Each of these chapels was opened by John Wesley himself, the latter in his 87th year. In the course of time each of these places of worship gave birth to other chapels in the surrounding areas, and it was from Cherry Street that the much loved Wesley Chapel, Constitution Hill, evolved in 1828, which in 1862 became the head of the new Birmingham (Wesley) Circuit. It was from this chapel that Aston Villa developed in 1850.

The original Aston Villa chapel, built at a cost of £600, must have been a small building for it was heated by means of one stove. Apparently it had no vestry for, until the erection of the present building in 1865, the trustees' meetings were usually held in a vestry at Wesley Chapel. The premises were somewhat enlarged in 1862 when a schoolroom was erected at a cost of £92.

The first reference to the new chapel was in April 1862, when a committee of the trustees was appointed to report on a suitable site. In the next year, the site was agreed upon and it was resolved that the new chapel should be Gothic in architecture, and that 200 free sittings should be provided for the poor. During this year, plans and estimates were invited for a building with and without galleries and with and without a spire.

From twelve estimates received it was decided to accept the one that cost £2,883, which included the erection of a spire and galleries. The work however, did not proceed as smoothly as the trustees wished, and a committee was appointed with the architect to visit the contractor but 'found that he was away supervising the building of another chapel. In his absence the committee took the opportunity to examine his yard and were struck by its inadequate resources for any large undertaking and in view of the rise in the cost of materials and a threatened strike of workmen, the trustees were advised not to ratify the contract' and another tender for £3,390 was accepted.

Councillor Naish laid a memorial stone in April 1864, and arrangements were made for the President of the Conference to open the new building on 10th May 1865. Unfortunately, further labour troubles arose and, owing to a carpenters' strike, the opening was postponed until 31st May. Another alteration in the arrangements is revealed by the somewhat laconic record that 'death having severed the engagement between the President of the Conference and this Trust' the Rev. Dr Osborn was requested to preach in his stead. Special preachers during the series of opening services in addition to Dr Osborne included Revs. W. Suther M.A., E. E. Jenkins, W. Cattle, C. Vince and Dr Waddy, and the collections amounted to £370.

In those days pew rents were an important item in the church's revenue, and rentals were fixed on a sliding scale from

3/- per quarter per sitting for the centre pews to 1/- per quarter in the fourth row of the galleries. Donors of £50 and upwards were entitled, according to their contributions, to a first selection of pews, donors of the same amount balloting for priority of choice. Ministers' widows were entitled to the next selection and the remainder of donors and pew owners who required whole pews balloted for priority of choice. These being supplied, those requiring individual sittings were selected by ballot. In 1878, the pew rents had reached the total of £284 per annum.

The difference in outlook of the early trustees and their conception of the functions of the church compared with present day ideas is clearly revealed by some of the decisions made in those early days. In 1869, two ladies requested the use of the schoolroom in order to give instruction in physical culture. This was refused. Two other ladies, who had already given physical culture instruction without permission, were waited upon by the minister and treasurer of the trust and warned not to do it again.

In 1870, a request was made for the use of the school for a proposed amateur choral society. The trustees required further particulars as to the nature of the society and the character of the meeting, which would be considered at a special trustee's meeting. There is however, no further reference to the society or the special meeting. A few years later, the trustees sanctioned the occasional use of an anthem, either at morning or evening service, provided that at least two succeeding services were without an anthem. It was further decided that no new tune should be introduced into the service until it had been sung at least twice by the choir in place of a chant or anthem.

In December 1870, a new organ was erected at the west end of the chapel at a cost of £400. It was opened free of debt. Indecently, when the Sunday School Committee heard that a new organ was proposed, a request was made to the trustees for the harmonium which hitherto been used in the chapel, to be presented to the Sunday school. The organ committee offered the instrument to the Sunday school for £15 and the offer was declined with thanks.

In 1871, it was decided to purchase two houses in Lozells Road adjoining the church premises. A large vestry was built in the garden of the first house and a chancel erected over the vestry to contain the organ, which was removed from the rear of the chapel.

By March 1883, the debt on the chapel amounted to £2,630 and a few years later, as a fine act of faith, it was decided to raise £4,000, £1,500 to be used for the reduction of debt and £2,500 to be applied to building and furnishing new Sunday schools. The need for the latter had become all too apparent as it had been impossible to accommodate the children of the district, who would have attended Sunday school.

As early as 1866 the Annual Report of the Sunday School stated 'during the last eighteen months there has been erected within half-a-mile of this place at least eighty houses, and if we only calculate three children to a house (which we think a fair average) that gives a total of 240 children who ought to attend a Sabbath School.'

In 1897, it was decided to purchase a new organ at a cost of £700 plus £150 for the old instrument. The organ was opened in the presence of a great congregation by Mr C. W. Perkins, City Organist of Birmingham, and the dedicatory service conducted by the President of the Conference, Rev. W. L. Watkinson (the famous Methodist preacher). In the following year a staircase was erected from the entrance to the large vestry to the choir stalls.

In 1905, the church was closed for one month for the installation of electric light and ventilating fans, re-heating, re-flooring and painting at a cost of £470, and in 1911 electric light was installed in the Sunday school and classrooms.

In March 1917, it was learned with regret that the mother church of Aston Villa - Wesley Chapel, Constitution Hill - was about to be closed and the trustees sent a message of invitation to the remaining members and arranged for the memorial brasses to be fixed in Aston Villa.

July 1919 saw the installation of an electric blower in the organ at a cost of £140, the amount being generously assured by the Choir Committee. In March 1921, it was decided to take advantage of the new Church Leasehold Enfranchisement Act to obtain the freehold of that portion of the premises held on lease. An interest free loan was granted by the Methodist Chapel Committee, and in 1934 the final instalment was repaid, which secured the freehold of all land on which the church property stands.

In November 1925, the alteration and extension of the choir stalls was approved at a cost of £190, and in November 1928 the whole of the inside of the school premises was redecorated by a band of voluntary workers without cost to the trustees.

For many years it was felt that the two separate entrances to the north and south aisles of the church mitigated against the fellowship of the whole congregation. In June 1934, the church was re-opened after the removal of the rear pews and the building of the present Crush Hall with its central entrance. At the same time, a new system of heating and electric lighting was installed and three stained glass windows were placed in the Crush Hall and a new communion table and chairs were given as memorials to devoted members of the church who had passed away.

Aston Villa had been fortunate in that since 1881, Handsworth College had been in the Wesley Circuit. From that date it had the advantage of frequent services of some of Methodism's most famous theologians and preachers. These included the Revs Robert Young, F. W. Macdonald, Thomas Allen, Silvester Whitehead, J. G. Tasker, W. T. Davison, F. Platt, W. W. Holdsworth, W. F. Lofthouse, H. Bett, Dr Howard and the present staff of the college. Aston Villa was the nearest large chapel in the early days of the college and, when not engaged in preaching, the students worshipped there. Among the favourite preachers of the students was the Rev. J. E. Clapham who, whilst the Minister of Aston Villa, was also the first secretary of the College Committee.

Most members of Aston Villa have often met people who were under the impression that the church was named after the famous football club. The position is actually the reverse. The original club was formed by members of the Aston Villa Bible Class. A memorable service was held in May 1935, when the chairman of Aston Villa Football Club, several players and the secretary took part in the devotions.

Since the erection of the building in 1865 there has been one problem that recurred with unfailing regularity to the present day – the maintenance and repair of the roof and steeple. For many years repairs were necessary after every severe storm. The position was seriously aggravated by the effect of bomb-blast during the late war. So serious had the condition become that it was imperative last year that the whole of the roof be stripped and retiled after faulty timbers had been renewed. It was also necessary to remove the spire in order to save the recurring expense of maintenance.

Although the War Damage Commission has given some relief, the major portion of the cost is the responsibility of the trustees, and the Centenary Celebrations commence with commitments of £1,000. The trustees confidently believe that by the end of the celebrations old and new friends of Aston Villa, by their generosity, will ensure that the great work that has been and is being done and will be carried on into the second century unhampered by financial burdens in order that the minister, leaders and church officials alike may concentrate on the things of the Spirit and the extension of the Kingdom of God.

Aston Villa Methodist Church closed in 1962 and the building was sold to the New Testament Church of God. In 2008, the old building was demolished and a new building opened on the site in 2009. This building hosted one of the Methodist ordination services at the Birmingham Methodist Conference in June 2014.

Kathleen Collman

REFLECTIONS FROM THE ORDINATION SERVICE AT THE NEW TESTAMENT CHURCH OF GOD

Handsworth, 29th June 2014

When I became President of Conference in 2011, I knew immediately that to preside at an ordination would be one of the special moments. I was not wrong and nor has that specialness gone when, since that first service at Chester Cathedral, I have subsequently presided at Truro Methodist Church (best remembered or forgotten for a mishap with the communion wine!) and this year at the New Testament Church of God, Handsworth. This year's service however, had a very special significance for me as it took place in the circuit (Birmingham Wesley) in which I grew up and where both my parents and grandparents were actively involved: in my parents' case at Somerset Road, and in my grandparents' at Lozells, just a stone's throw away from the church in which the ordination took place. When I was a child the New Testament Church of God was, of course, Aston Villa Methodist Church from which the famous football team originated. I remember my father coming home one Sunday evening from church and complaining that if the local preacher (from Aston Villa Methodist Church) had said a little more about God and a little less about football he'd have been better pleased! Nevertheless, my father and grandfather before him were loyal Villa supporters even if they only attended once a year. Following their advice that there was only one team worth supporting, I have been a loyal Villa fan ever since, watching them many times more than once a year, although at present that is about my average. So the ordination was a poignant moment of gratitude to my parents for the faith in which I was nurtured, of the thought of their amazement and godly joy that I was standing where I was, of my love of sport that has given me both joy and heartache, of the universal church represented by the President Designate of the Methodist Church in Hong Kong, whom I had met here only a few weeks before, and of the whole company of heaven including so many ministers in that and other circuits throughout Methodism. Most of all, I tried always to remember throughout, that the service was not about the past, however special, but about the present and future and so with 'the great congregation ascribing salvation to Jesus our king' prayed that the Holy Spirit would come afresh on those ordained for the office and work of a presbyter in the church of God. May it be so and to God alone be the glory in the church and in Christ Jesus now and forever.

Rev. Leo Osborn

Chair of Newcastle upon Tyne District
Former President of Conference
Standing below the Aston Villa Football Club memorial plaque.

The plaque has the image of the Aston Villa Football Club coat of arms, below which is the following inscription:

> THIS SITE IS THE BIRTHPLACE OF
> ASTON VILLA FOOTBALL CLUB
> WHICH WAS FORMED IN 1874
> BY FOUR MEMBERS OF THE
> ASTON VILLA METHODIST CHURCH
> A BUILDING WHICH STOOD ON THIS SITE
> FROM 1865-2007

A summer activity of the Aston Villa Wesleyan Church Bible Class was to play cricket. In 1874 some members of the cricket team decided they needed a winter activity to keep themselves fit. Four members of the cricket team, Walter Price, William Scattergood, Jack Hughes and Frederick Matthews decided to start a football club. They formed a committee and opened a bank account in the name of the football club that became the foundation of the Aston Villa Football Club.

Foundation stones of the Aston Villa Wesleyan Church preserved in the foyer of the New Testament Church of God, Handsworth.

Aston Villa Methodist Church Foundation Stone, November 23, 1887

Aston Villa Methodist Church Foundation Stone, November 23, 1887

New Testament Church of God, Handsworth

The New Testament Church of God is a newly built church on the site of the Aston Villa Wesleyan/Methodist Church

Leo Osborn
Donald H. Ryan

BLACKHEATH AND HALESOWEN CIRCUIT – SNIPPETS OF HISTORY

Halesowen and Blackheath

The Methodist churches in Blackheath and Halesowen townships from 1878 up until 2008 were formed into separate Methodist circuits, so each have their own story to tell. This is an attempt to amalgamate snippets of history.

Both townships were strong centres of Primitive Methodism in the mid-nineteenth century, but there is evidence of Wesleyanism in Halesowen town centre, a cause that possibly converted to the Methodist New Connexion. In Blackheath there was a strong Methodist New Connexion cause and two smaller ones.

HALESOWEN

John Wesley visited Halesowen on 19th March 1770 and preached on Dungeon Head, High Street, Cradley (near to St. Peter's Church). He wrote in his journal, "I rode to Craidley. Here also the multitude of people obliged me to stand abroad, although the north wind whistled round my head." A society was formed there in 1766 and its descendant meets today at Overend Methodist Mission.

The Methodist churches in the Cradley area are not members of the Birmingham Methodist District. John Wesley was in Halesowen again on 13th July 1783 when he visited The Leasowes, the home of William Shenstone, the poet and landscape gardener. In a letter Wesley said of The Leasowes that he doubted that it be exceeded in all Europe." Cradley appears on a Dudley Wesleyan plan of 1812 and Halesowen is recorded in the Stourbridge Wesleyan Circuit in 1829 as having one member, but that same year the membership had increased to eight.

Rev. William Jones

The prosperity of the circuit was clouded in 1835-6, when dissension took place over the formation of a theological institution. Many of the members with their chapels joined the Methodist New Connexion. The circuit minutes record "a very promising cause at Halesowen has never been replaced." This cause was very likely the one that met in Brook Road (off Birmingham Street), Halesowen, and they eventually built their new chapel, the Zion Chapel, in 1842, in Stourbridge Road.

Primitive Methodist Church

The earliest Primitive Methodist cause in Halesowen began at Cherry Tree Lane, Hayley Green. A group of missioners from Lye were holding a meeting on the village green. Josiah Male was on the top of his haystack. He listened to their message and was so moved he came down and was converted. He invited the missioners into his cottage and so began our Hasbury Society. It first appears on the Dudley Circuit plan of November to January 1832–33 and is styled as Hailey Green. One service was held each Sunday at 2.30pm. The first chapel was built in 1837, on the edge of a field called the Red Leasowes. A new chapel was built in 1865. In 1946, land adjoining the chapel was purchased and the new chapel erected here in 1970. This chapel was considerably extended in 1985. It was replaced by the present church, which opened in 2000.

Hasbury Methodist Church

The first Primitive Methodist chapel in the centre of Halesowen was built at the bottom of Birmingham Street in 1848. On 30th March 1851, there were 110 adults and 81 children: 140 and 77 respectively came to the afternoon service and 150 adults attended the evening service.

A new chapel was built in 1868 and the minister, Rev. William Wright, wrote in the *Primitive Methodist Magazine* "A splendid chapel is in the course of erection. The trustees have worked well in raising £100 for the site of land and £50 more at the stone laying. The chapel will be the finest and neatest building in the town. Our prospects here are bright and cheery."

Hasbury Methodist Church

A notable member of this society was Rev. William Jones, who was born at Hawne Bank in 1834. He worked in a nail shop as a young man and entered the ministry in 1855. As a young man it was said of him, "That chap bay arf saft. He gos and praiches to the cabbages." He was known as "The Enchanting Gospel Orator" and the power of his preaching was such that he could hold the attention of huge congregations for several hours. He was appointed President of the Primitive Methodist Conference at the time of Queen Victoria's Diamond Jubilee and attended a banquet at Buckingham Palace. He described to one of the Parsons family the ruched black silk dress the Queen wore. He served in twenty circuits and then returned to Halesowen for one year to serve as minister, before retiring in the place of his birth.

Another well-known preacher who started his days at Birmingham Street Society was Rev. Walter Tildesley. He emigrated to America in 1923 and had an outstanding ministry. For the last ten years of his ministry he served a large Methodist church near the White House in Washington DC.

Shenstone Primitive Methodist Church was built at the instigation of John Jones of Prospect Place, a well-known local preacher and member of the Birmingham Street Church. The church closed in 1959 and was demolished due to road widening and creation of the Shenstone Island.

Short Cross Primitive Methodist Church had its beginnings in 1867, when four members started meeting in a house in the Gibbet Lane area, now Alexandra Road. Their driving force was a Mr and Mrs William Southwell. They sought permission to build a schoolroom. On 12th March 1867, a piece of land was purchased for £44.4.0d and the first building was erected in 1868. It was replaced in 1891. In 1934, a new church was built at a cost of £2,000. The beautiful peace window, which is also the 1914-18 War Memorial, was transferred to the present church and forms a central position above the communion table. The former church was used as the schoolroom until a new schoolroom was built in 1979. An extension was built in 1995 and called '1868 room' because it was built on the original foundations of that year.

Short Cross Primitive Methodist Church, 1891

Down the years other churches have been built at Hayseech, 1870, and Romsley, 1870, with a new building in 1930. For a time the circuit owned Caleb Bloomer's Islington Ragged Schools in Stourbridge Road, which had a baptismal font and was also run as a church. There were also causes at Lower Hagley, Shelton and Illey. All of these Primitive Methodist churches were members of the Dudley Circuit, with 17 other churches ranging from Oldbury to Brierley Hill. As the number of churches multiplied, the Brierley Hill Circuit was formed from the Dudley Circuit, the Old Hill Circuit from the Brierley Hill Circuit in 1867, and the Hasbury and Halesowen Circuit in 1878. In 1889, the Blackheath and Quinton Circuit was formed. In 1901, the Blackheath and Langley Green Primitive Methodist Circuit was formed.

BLACKHEATH

Keckmoor is mentioned in the Dudley Primitive Methodist Circuit minute book of 1839, having a society of 17 members 'on trial'. The identity of this place is Cakemore. However, a resolution was passed in 1850 'That Keckmoor come off the plan'. To the north side of Blackheath, in 1842, a society was formed with eight members known as 'Rowley and Perry's Lake'. That same year, Rev. Richard Ward was appointed to the Dudley Circuit and on his first visit to the society walked down Rowley Hill on his way to the preaching house and began talking to several families. Some people were alarmed by his approach, leaving their houses and running into their nail shops. Richard Ward wrote in his journal "This is a large place but the inhabitants are extremely ignorant and wicked." When he reached the preaching house he spoke to a small argumentative congregation. This visit was followed by other visits by Richard Ward and other travelling preachers and in March 1848, Rowley and Blackheath was placed on the Dudley Circuit plan. Though no record of numbers has been kept, the society sent a contribution of five shillings to the circuit. From this time onwards, the society prospered and on 5th August 1850 the foundation stone at Blackheath was laid. The resulting church was built where the present Central Methodist Church stands, at a cost of £340. That building was replaced in 1902 by High Street Methodist Church with seating for 900. In the years that followed, the main interest of the Blackheath Society was in local affairs. Blackheath itself was developing quickly and had already become predominantly a township. People, who were once farm workers in the surrounding countryside, were joining the industrial trend and came to Blackheath area to work in the local nail and chain making industries or to work in the quarries and mines of the Rowley Hills. During these years other Primitive Methodist societies were being formed in the area.

One such society was Long Lane, the predecessor of Crossway. In 1866, a church was erected just off Long Lane in New England at the cost of £360. This church was replaced by the Long Lane building in 1908. In December 1877, it was passed 'That Blackheath friends have permission to purchase land for a small chapel at Cockshutts'. The Cocksheds Chapel was erected in 1884. It cost £350 and seated 200 people. Another small society developed at Hurst Green, originally meeting in a small wooden summerhouse. However, in 1881 they erected a small brick building, which cost only £65 and seated 100 people. The present church was built in 1936.

At the commencement of the section on Halesowen, mention is made of the Methodist New Connexion, a separate denomination from Primitive Methodism. Blackheath had three Methodist New Connexion churches. In 1840, in a cottage in Yew Tree Lane, a society was formed which then moved on to hold services in Dr Beasley's coach house in Siviters Lane. In 1849, the society purchased for £5 land in The Causeway where they built the Ebenezer Chapel, which opened in 1850. The foundation stone of a new chapel, Birmingham Road Methodist (still standing but not now owned by the Methodist Church), was laid in October 1905. A contemporary newspaper report indicated that all 900 seats were filled at the opening ceremony, with another thousand or so people unable to get in. Malt Mill Lane Church was built in 1894, Whiteheath in 1842. This building was replaced with a new church in 1956. In 1995, High Street, Cocksheds, Malt Mill Lane and Whiteheath premises were closed and the congregations amalgamated with Birmingham Road and became Central Methodist Church. For a time the church worshipped at Birmingham Road premises, whilst the High Street premises were demolished and the new Central Methodist Church was built on the site. This is where the congregation now worships.

Blackheath Central Methodist Church

One other Methodist church still remains in Blackheath: the Heath Street Independent Methodist Church, founded in 1867. It was a Wesleyan Reform Union Society, which became the United Methodist Free Church Association. At the turn of the century, the society applied to become a member of the Blackheath Primitive Methodist Circuit and was accepted in 1904. The church was replaced in 1976 by a new building owing to road widening. The church is not now a member of a circuit.

In 2008, the Blackheath and Halesowen Methodist circuits amalgamated, so societies that had been members of the same circuit in the 1800's were once again members of the same circuit. Long may it continue.

(Acknowledgements to Anthony Page and Graham Hadley for information on Blackheath Methodism.)

David L. Eades

50TH ANNIVERSARY OF THE BUILDING OF BLACKWOOD METHODIST CHURCH

2015 was our 50th anniversary celebration year with a big programme of events. Each month we welcomed a guest minister for Sunday worship, including many of our former ministers. Special services were arranged, such as one for those who were married at Blackwood.

In January 2015, the year started with our Covenant Service on Sunday 4th. A special community weekend in September marked the actual anniversary of the church's opening. Many social events were held, such as a concert by the Streetly Singers, a strawberry tea and fete, a fish and chip supper and a Blackwood history slide show, plus a pudding tasting and a quiz event.

The following article was written in 1971 from the experiences of people closely involved, six years after the new church was dedicated. It can be seen from the article that after the church was dedicated on September 11th 1965 it quickly became a spiritual and social centre for the area. Today, with its newly updated facilities, the church plays host to some 17 organisations that meet here on a regular basis. It is our big family.

The Origins Of Blackwood Methodist Church 1955 - 2015

The Methodist church at Streetly was established early in the twentieth century, but as the population began to grow nearer to the Chester Road (A452), some of the Streetly people thought another church might be necessary. There was consideration of a site on the Chester Road for a new church but nothing developed.

One of those who foresaw the need for another society was Mr B. T. Nicholas. His daughter, Margery, started a Sunday school before the war to save people travelling to Streetly. Her first Sunday school met in a room in a house in Bridle Lane. The room was bare except for a table. 12 children arrived for the first session. The little ones were put on the table and the bigger ones sat on the floor. Margery armed herself with materials she could carry in a rucksack. When a new baby arrived in the household where the Sunday school met, Miss Nicholas and her charges had to move on. For a while they met in the holiday camp in Bridle Lane, then in the council school on Foley Road. Roads were not as plentiful then and children often had to cross fields to get to Sunday school. The next venue was in a house on the Chester Road, called Bethany. The owner made a room and an organ available. One Harvest Thanksgiving service was held in the garden. Towards the end of the Second World War, the National Fire Service vacated a hut at the junction of Thornhill Road and Chester Road so the Sunday school moved yet again, this time to a place of its own. Unfortunately, the result was that the Bridle Lane children gradually left and the new Congregational Church in Westwood Road agreed to take over the Sunday school work and Miss Nicholas with it.

Practically ten years had elapsed when Margery Nicholas had a chance conversation at the bus stop with a Mrs Nicholas of Bridle Lane, who had memories of the earlier Sunday school efforts. By that time, the population west of Streetly village had continued to grow and the two ladies felt that the need for a Sunday school was just as great as it had been a decade before. The matter was put to the leaders at Streetly, who resolved to find a site to erect a suitable building for Sunday school work in the Bridle Lane area. Correspondence was opened with the local authority. The Bridle Lane residents were anxious for speedier action and the Senior Steward at Streetly, John Coates, met residents and decided to make use of the dining room in the Bridle Lane holiday camp, which was not in use in the winter months.

On 2nd October 1955, the first meeting with 76 children between the ages of 3 and 13 years was held. By February 1956, John Coates was able to report to the circuit stewards "Since October some organisation has been attempted and we now have a Beginners Section, a Primary Section with 5 teachers and a General Superintendent (myself). All the departments and classes are held in the one hall, screened with what we could find on the premises. Conditions are far from ideal, but we feel worthwhile." At the request of interested adults an experimental evening service was proposed, conducted by John Coates. It was held at the holiday camp on 20th November 1955. 17 people were present and they signed their names. Spring 1956 meant the holiday camp reverted to its normal use but the group continued to meet in a house. The society enjoyed the support of Rev. Clifford Booker, the minister in charge of Four Oaks and Streetly churches. A search for new premises continued. At circuit level there were doubts about the future of the independent society. As the then Birmingham (Sutton Park) Circuit Superintendent, Rev. John T. Jones put it "The Circuit hesitated about supporting work in the Blackwood area for good reasons." At the time, development at Falcon Lodge had prior claims and the size of the Sutton Park Circuit raised doubts about adding new churches west of Chester Road. The possibility of the Kingstanding Circuit undertaking the work was considered, but the value of the close alliance with and interest of Streetly in the new group finally overcame the objections.

The big breakthrough came when a hut became available in Mere Green. Mr Nicholas provided money towards the purchase of a site and the hut was brought to the woods at Blackwood and erected by John Coates and other willing helpers. On 27th July 1957, Lady Bennett formally opened the hut and a procession, appropriately led by the choir of Sunday school children, entered the church that was then dedicated by the Circuit Superintendent.

The Blackwood Society, with its 11 members, had a permanent home and, in ones and twos, newcomers arrived to add their contribution. Some were Methodists who had moved into the area and others joined from other traditions. Sunday services and house groups continued; uniformed organisations were started. A youth club and the Sunday school flourished. Accommodation was limited to the one main room. A much smaller room was added in 1959. Despite these handicaps, plus no flush toilet facilities and a cold water supply from a tap near the road, the society developed a lively range of activities. Sunday school outings became virtually a church outing. The Summer Gala in the woods around the hut attracted much interest. Ultimately the point was reached when no more people could be seated at the traditional Harvest Supper, prepared and served by the men. The Women's Fellowship arranged a Christmas Fair and every method was used to raise money for the new building, which seemed to be some distance in the future. Meanwhile the Sunday school, the original reason for the building of Blackwood, multiplied and every Sunday morning the able-bodied men moved swiftly into action at the end of the service to erect partition boards to make possible a division of the hut for departments in the afternoon. Sunday school anniversaries presented a problem because they always attracted a larger than usual congregation, so the practice had to be started to have two Sundays with identical services to meet the demand for seats.

In the summer of 1962, enough musically minded members were available to form a small choir. A few had considerable experience but a number had never sung in a choir before though were willing to have a try. We obtained tune books and used those as our basic music until the subscriptions paid by the choristers raised enough money to buy anthems. The beginning was, of necessity, modest, but with the co-operation of local preachers the choir provided extra music for the festivals such as Christmas, Easter and Harvest and practically every recruit to Blackwood who appeared with a tune book in their hands was added to our number so that we felt strong enough to compete with other established churches in the 1965 Eisteddfod.

The tradition of house meetings lasted long after the hut was opened. Discussion groups continued and throughout the winter the choir met for practice in the warm and commodious lounge of the Coates' home in Chester Road. Most smaller church meetings, such as the leaders' meetings, were held in members houses rather than in the austere surroundings of the hut that had to be heated with fan heaters and electric fires. The intimacy of meetings of all descriptions in domestic surroundings made some members wonder if something valuable would be lost when the new building eventually came into use but there was never any question that a permanent church building must be achieved. Pleasant though the small gatherings of friends might be, everyone worked with a vision of a growing society, which would be bigger and greater than anything that could exist in the hut.

Funds from the Connexion and the circuit together with about £6,000 raised by Blackwood members allowed the trustees to make active preparations for a church building. Len Trickett must have been one of the proudest and most thankful members of the Blackwood Society when he moved his men onto the site to commence operations. The foundations were laid and the sun shone warmly on the large gathering, which stood round the foundation stone laid by Mr T. D. Nicholas on Saturday 4th September 1964. After the ceremony, members and friends went to Streetly Church where tea was provided and a Service of Thanksgiving followed, at which the combined Streetly and Blackwood choirs had the privilege of singing Stanford's great setting of the *Te Deum*.

Work on the building proceeded all winter in the hope that the church would be ready by the autumn of 1965. Appropriately again, the Sunday school had first use of the new building. Construction was sufficiently advanced for the Sunday school anniversary services to be held in the new hall in the spring of 1965. The hall was packed, a foretaste of future Sunday school anniversaries. Finally the whole church was ready and the chairman of the district, Rev. Wilfred Bridge, came to Blackwood on Saturday 11th September 1965, to dedicate the building for public worship. Representatives of other denominations took part in the service, which attracted enough people to fill both the church and the hall.

Since then, Rev. Clifford Booker, who gave his help to the first people interested, and Rev. Bernard Howell, who worked hard and successfully in the first years of the hut, have been able to return and lead worship in the buildings that fell to Rev. Clifford Hardy to take in his charge. For years, the need for a new church attracted everyone's attention but by 1965, with the physical building in being, the people of Blackwood had to answer the fundamental question, "What to do with it?" After much discussion we decided to challenge all our people to offer their time and talents, as well as money, to the church to enrich its spiritual, pastoral and social life. The campaign in November 1965, guided by the Methodist Stewardship Organisation, literally touched hundreds of people. Every organisation of the church drew benefit from the campaign and in some cases Blackwood has become a valued social centre in what for many is a rootless district. Some people find Blackwood meetings, not necessarily the specifically religious ones, a great source of comfort and the outreach of the Blackwood Society, evident in the help given to poverty areas in Birmingham and overseas, is equally real in providing a Christian approach in the locality.

In six years, practically all activities have doubled. Church membership has doubled. There are two youth clubs and two women's meetings where there was only one. More children attend Sunday school and the society takes a much greater share of circuit responsibilities. This trend is roughly opposite to the national trend in church life and the church members have constantly to examine the purpose of the church and its role in the community. It is evident that in our rapidly changing society where certainty to some is uncertainty to others, the church means many different things to many different people. Having become well established in the area the members of Blackwood are seeking to find the best ways to serve.

The pioneering visionaries who started the 1939 Sunday school and the 1955 holiday camp school were faithful workers who led the way to the founding of Blackwood Methodist Church. The present generation, following the vision of the earlier pioneers, must now embrace the on-going mission of

Blackwood Methodist Church to be a spiritual and community heart of the area.

With thanks to C. H. Smith, 12th February 1971.

John Harden

BRISTOL ROAD AND NORTHFIELD WESLEYAN CHURCHES, BIRMINGHAM

Introduction

The story of Northfield Methodist Church, Chatham Road, is really the story of four churches.

In 2014, the present building celebrated its Silver Jubilee following redevelopment in 1989 after the demolition of the 1956 church. This large 1956 church, with its extensive suite of ancillary premises, had become too expensive to maintain so the decision was taken to demolish the church and redevelop the back premises. The 1956 building had been erected to replace the original Northfield Church (1899) and the Bristol Road, Benacre Road (1834) church. The Bristol Road Church had been destroyed by enemy action on the night of 29/30th October 1940. This article tells the story of those two early churches.

BRISTOL ROAD METHODIST CHURCH, BENACRE STREET

The Bristol Road Wesleyan Methodist Society was started in 1832 by a Mr Wright and first met in a room over a shop in Spring Street (off Spring Vale). In 1834, the society moved to a chapel, a converted building in Bell Barn Road (off Lee Bank Road), which was later sold to the Welsh Baptists. As early as 1836, it was decided that larger and better accommodation was required and the trustees were empowered to obtain a suitable site and raise funds. After protracted negotiations between the trustees, the occupier, William Guest, and the owner, Sir Thomas Gooch, a site on the corner of Benacre Street and Bristol Road (about where Bristol Street Motors now is) was acquired in 1843 for £1,150. An appeal was made to the circuit for support but other financial commitments meant it was unable to respond immediately. However, in 1850, architects were invited to submit plans for the new building and, after due consideration and emendation to suit the financial guidelines, the plans of Wilson and Fuller (London and Bath) were accepted. The tender of Thomas Upton (Balsall Heath Road) was deemed satisfactory and building commenced, the foundation stone being laid on Monday March 21st 1853. The church opened on 18th January 1854, when the Rev. John Lomas, President of Conference, preached in the morning and the Rev. John Angell James of Carrs Lane Congregational Church in the evening. The chapel was built in the Gothic style, being 75 feet long and 48 feet wide, seating about 800 people, rising to 1200 when, in 1854, side galleries were added. The pews were rented but 350 seats were left free for 'the poor'. The chapel cost £3,652 and a harmonium was purchased for £36.14s. In 1865, an organ was installed and the schools enlarged. From 1872 to 1886, the Benacre schools were used as a Wesleyan day school and then continued under the control of the School Board until 1889. 22 foundation and memorial stones were laid on 26th October 1896 when the chapel was extended and renovated and the Sunday school rebuilt - a £6,200 ambitious scheme. The Rev. Hugh Price Hughes spoke at the evening public meeting. The new Sunday school was opened by the President of Conference, Rev. Dr Marshall Randles, and the Mayoress of West Bromwich on 24th May 1897, while yet another president, Rev. W. L. Watkinson, was present later in the year for the reopening of the renovated chapel. In 1908, over £600 was spent on a new organ and an electric blower was added later. The records note that professional organists valued it at £2,000.

The pew rent system brought in a goodly income until 1924, when all seats were designated as 'free and inappropriate'. In spite of difficulties during WW1, the church managed to balance its yearly accounts to enable the real work of the church to continue. The stonework had decayed so badly that in 1934/5 an exterior renovation scheme was undertaken and the organ overhauled at the cost of £535. The 1937/8 minutes record that the May synod was held in the church, a 'Talkie Cinema' installed and the gift of the Pershore Road manse received.

The church was the third in a line of churches —Wycliffe Baptist and St Luke's Anglican - on the right hand side of Bristol Road. The whole area consisted of small, dark back-to-back houses with tiny pocket-handkerchief gardens. Mrs Bassett Reed, wife of the last minister, remembered that "they were always clean and bright with flowers, and the people were wonderful." Church membership was around 200; average attendance at

Sunday school 250 and up to 300 attended the Band of Hope, often to see the 'sound films'. There was a children's Sunday evening service, a Cub group, a Men's Club and Women's Bright Hour. Guild and class meetings met regularly and open-air services accompanied by a harmonium were held. The Christmas morning breakfast was a highlight of the year, when 600 children enjoyed a good meal and entertainment before going home clutching a card, an orange and a new penny. The annual New Year's Eve Watch Night Service attracted hundreds to 'see the New Year in'. The church's life was vital, happy and rewarding, but when, in WW2, Birmingham became the target for German bombs, the Bristol Road church and the surrounding area became very vulnerable. On Saturday October 26th 1940, an incendiary bomb fell through the roof, hit a brass collection plate, bounced and burned harmlessly through the floor. However, during the night of 29/30th October, several fire and oil bombs set alight both the church and school premises and after 1½ hours only a smouldering ruin was left. There were 46 fires that night in Birmingham and the emergency services were stretched to the limit so there was no hope of saving the church. Again, Mrs Reed remembered that she, her husband and a little group of members joined together next morning for a short service in the ruins, 'a very moving, heart-rending occasion'. Mr Reed erected a large noticeboard on the outside of the ruins with the words 'The City of God remaineth', an indication of the spirit and faith of its members. Two weeks later, landmines fell in the same area, causing great damage and some casualties but the church, although the building was destroyed, continued to help people who had lost their homes. Wycliffe Baptist Church next door generously provided facilities for the services and work of the

Methodist Church, with the congregation meeting for several months in its Lower Lecture Hall before they joined up with the Methodist Church in Selly Park. At first, it was hoped to restore and rebuild the remaining building but further bomb damage nearby weakened it. Then, following serious consideration and consultation with the Baptist Church leaders about the spiritual needs of the neighbourhood and their own planned expansion, it was decided not to rebuild on the Benacre Street site, but to use war damage compensation, which legally had to be used for one set of church premises, elsewhere in the circuit. It was first suggested that this should be at Longbridge and the site was actually purchased, but at that time (1952) it was not felt opportune to build a large church there. With the expansion of Northfield that church had found that their existing building was now inadequate so it was decided a new church should be built on the land at Bristol Road South and Chatham Road, incorporating a memorial chapel with the rescued door arch of the Benacres Street church as an entrance. The 1953 Northfield March Quarterly Meeting passed a resolution to this effect and guaranteed to 'raise the sum of £7,500 for the Longbridge scheme' when that new church should be built. So closed one phase of the life of the Bristol Road church, but the spirit, hope, faith and vision of its members was to be perpetuated in the same way as its predecessor.

NORTHFIELD METHODIST CHURCH

The Home Office Ecclesiastical Returns for Northfield record that a Wesleyan chapel was built in 1841; however, the Worship Returns of the Worcester Diocese (16th November 1838) show that the first registration of a chapel for Methodist worship was made in 1838. The chapel in use at the time of the Religious Census of 1851 provided sittings for 120 people. The actual whereabouts of these chapels is a matter of debate. A Primitive Methodist chapel was registered for public worship by 1856. It was described as 'a building near the Bell Inn' and was possibly the former malt house later used by the Society of Friends, though a building on the site of the now demolished 'Travellers' Rest' public house was said to have been used by the 'Ranters', which was the early Primitive Methodists' nickname. So the very early history of Methodism in Northfield is full of fascinating hints but with a tantalising lack of definite facts. When we reach the end of the nineteenth century however, we are on firmer ground as reference can be made to Trust Minute Books.

The original site was purchased and a school chapel erected in the spring of 1899 'irregularly' - that is without the permission of Synod and Chapel Committee. The situation was regularised in 1902 and many money-raising efforts were held to pay off the debt to the members who had first bought the land. The whole enterprise cost £1,319. By 1906, the men's Sunday afternoon Bible class had grown so large that they needed a larger room and the members were even ready to pay the interest on the sum expended if the Trust would put up a new building or enlarge the vestry. Other organisations also felt the need for enlarged facilities so a new room and other renovations were carried out at a cost of £193.11s, which left the Trust Account in 1907 with a balance of 6s. 9d. In 1914, the chapel was licensed for the solemnisation of marriages. The 1918 Trustees Meeting Minutes recorded that a pipe organ had been installed and a communion table had been donated anonymously.

In 1923, the trustees authorised negotiations with Mr Ryland Smith to buy a plot of land adjacent to the chapel. Eventually, in 1925, 3723 square yards between the church's existing boundary and Maas Road was purchased by 'friends' to be used as the site for a new church, schools and tennis courts. Some trustees optimistically hoped for a new church within three years (1928).

1926 saw the gas lighting replaced by electricity, services being held in the Baptist church while the premises were redecorated, and brass plates in memory of two members placed in the church. When Bristol Road was widened the trustees realised that it provided a great opportunity to erect a wayside pulpit message - 'Jesus <u>shall</u> reign' - to attract people entering Birmingham from the south.

Northfield Methodist Church, 1926

A proposal to have it painted on the roof was rejected so slogans were placed along the fence by the side of the chapel for a short time. The Sunday school and Guild Room were used by Birmingham Education Committee to provide an extra temporary school. The church premises were renovated in 1940 and the land divided into allotments, which were rented out at 10/- a year. During WW2, services were brought forward to 5.30pm to avoid having to 'black out' the church, and the schoolroom was used as a canteen and rest centre. Following the blitzing of the Bristol Road church, it was suggested that its electric organ blower might be repaired for use at Northfield but it was not suitable.

During the 1930's and 1940's, various offers were made for the land that the church owned and, with the building of the new church in mind, the trustees looked at alternative sites in the area. They were particularly interested in 'one at the corner of South Road and Bristol Road which they were offered at a reasonable price, £2,700'. The existing site was valued at £11,500 so the temptation was to sell it and buy the other, using the balance to build a new church. However, on the advice of Dr E. Benson Perkins (Secretary of the Chapel Committee), the offer was turned down as he considered the Chatham Road site to be superior, meaning the existing church could be used while a new one was being built, as indeed happened. A joint meeting of the leaders and trustees on Wednesday June 26th 1946 discussed the future of the church and felt that, because of post-war conditions, a new church was very much in the future. It was urgent to have a resident minister in charge of Northfield to build up the existing church. This request was granted and Rev. Kenneth Richardson was appointed to have pastoral oversight of the Northfield and Longbridge churches.

In 1948, the church launched an appeal for £1,000 to renovate and beautify the existing buildings. The organ was moved to the side, the pulpit put on a central dais, choir stalls erected, the plain glass window replaced by a stained glass one, new communion furniture and plate purchased and blue carpet and curtains added. The church's Jubilee and the reopening services took place on the 10th September 1949. There were now so many scholars in the Sunday school that all the buildings and even the church itself, had to be used, with special Jubilee Anniversary services being held in May 1950. It soon became obvious, as the size of the congregation and all the organisations increased, that the existing premises were quite inadequate to cope with the expansion of the Northfield area. So, in 1953, following the decision not to rebuild the Bristol Road Church on the Benacre Road site, Northfield Church submitted an account of its needs to the circuit.

In due course, war damage compensation of £57,000 was granted to it to build a new church. An appeal for £12,000 was made to supplement the war damage compensation, so that an impressive church and suite of premises could be erected. The architects were J.P. Osborne and Son (Birmingham) and, after various adaptations, plans were drawn and the builders, Thomas Lowe and Sons Ltd., were instructed, their tender being £61,883. The President of Conference, Rev. W. Russell Shearer, laid the first foundation stone on Saturday November 13th 1954 at 3.00pm.

The two earlier churches now came together to work, pray and plan for an exciting future, pooling their experiences, their faith and their vision to continue the mission of being 'a caring church'. Saturday October 6th 1956 saw the opening and dedication of the new Bristol Road Methodist Church, Northfield, thus keeping the names of both churches alive.

E. Dorothy Graham

FOUR OAKS METHODIST CHURCH, SUTTON COLDFIELD, IN THE BIRMINGHAM SUTTON PARK CIRCUIT

Early Methodism In Four Oaks

Methodism in Four Oaks did not start with the building of the present church in 1903 on the corner of Four Oaks Road and Lichfield Road. Wesleyan Methodist evangelical preaching started when Francis Asbury of Great Barr established services in a cottage at Hill Hook in 1765. The cottage was situated near to where Blake Street Station stands today, in the home of his great friend, Edward Hand. Francis Asbury spent his last night locally with Edward before departing to become the founding father and bishop of the Methodist Church in North America. Edward Hand and his family were the objects of persecution because they were Methodists. On two

Edward Hand's house at Hill Hook

occasions neighbours set fire to their house. Having been granted a dissenters' licence by the Sutton Coldfield Justices on 7th October 1785, they were given notice to quit their house by Michaelmas Day 1787. Edward Hand and his family were evicted and their furniture put out on to the street. Despite this tragic situation Edward Hand continued to hold meetings in the area until about 1794. The Countess of Huntingdon's Connection established a cause during the 1770's in cottages in Belwell Lane, which were rented to the Wesleyan Methodists from 1794. The Wesleyan Methodists later purchased the site and built a chapel in 1799. The property was eventually sold to the Rector of Sutton in 1853 to be used as a dame school. The property was in due course demolished to make way for a Waitrose store. A Bible, including the Apocrypha, printed in 1707 and given to this chapel in 1837, is now on display in Four Oaks Methodist Church. Methodist services were also held in a cottage in Long Lane, Hill Hook from 1847 to 1868. During the 1880's the Walsall Wesleyan Circuit preaching plan shows an entry of services in a cottage at the junction of Walsall Road and Belwell Lane.

A HISTORY OF THE FOUR OAKS WESLEYAN METHODIST BUILDING

In 1880, Four Oaks racecourse was built, running around the Bracebridge end between Lichfield Road, Four Oaks Road and Sutton Park. The first race was in 1881, with the Grand National being run there later that year. When the racecourse closed in 1890, new roads were constructed and large houses were built to house the industrialists of Birmingham and the Black Country.

The coming of the railway in 1865 also encouraged development in the area.

A group of gentlemen saw the need for a Methodist church in the neighbourhood. After much debate they decided to acquire the land at the corner of Four Oaks Road and Lichfield Road. This was a step of great faith, as no Methodist society existed in the area at the time. The architects appointed by the newly formed trustees were Crouch and Butler. The cost of building was £10,000, which was raised by friends and an appeal to the people in the neighbourhood. The stone laying ceremony was on 22nd October 1902 at 4:00pm and was followed a year later by the opening on 6th October 1903 by Mr A. J. Webb 'amid rain and blustery weather'. At the time of the opening only the nave of the church, which served as chapel and school, had been built. These early premises soon proved inadequate and a further

£4,000 was raised to complete the building with transepts, vestry and tower. The schoolrooms were opened in 1909 and all was completed by 1910. The caretaker's cottage was built early on and the manse constructed in 1913 to house the first resident minister. The manse was erected following a gift from Mr G. E.

Lowe of £1,000. The whole building was faced with Weldon stone and roofed with Colleyweston stone slate. The church is built in a mixed Perpendicular, Gothic and Arts & Craft design.

Four Oaks Wesleyan Methodist Church became known as the 'Non-conformist Cathedral of the Midlands' and was one of the most beautiful Wesleyan Methodist churches. Separate gifts provided the stained glass window in the chancel, the communion table and chairs, the font and the pulpit with a beautiful panel representing Christ as the Good Shepherd.

In common with churches of many denominations at the time 'seat rents' were charged at 2s 6d per quarter and this raised £54 in 1904. The practice was stopped when pews replaced the seats in 1930. Membership grew steadily and activities thrived. The two manual organ, built by Norman and Beard, which is in use today, was installed in 1914. War work was tackled, including the formation of the 'ladies sewing meeting' to make items of clothing for 'soldiers at the front'. A plaque in the nave commemorates those men of the church who died during the war.

During the 1920's and 1930's the church seemed too far from the houses being built in the Mere Green area and membership did not grow very much. However, to some these were exciting times; a gas ring was provided for the kitchen, a microphone, amplifier and loudspeaker were installed and the present oak pews replaced the original chairs. It was during this time that the Boy Scout Group and Girl Guide Company were formed.

In 1940, a bomb fell 50 yards away but did little damage to the church. This prompted the temporary removal of the stained glass window, which was stored in the boiler room for safety. Evacuees from Coventry stayed on the premises for a while.

In 1947 it was agreed to purchase an electric fire for the church parlour (now the Bennett Room). A suggestion was made to improve the acoustics in the church by fixing copper wires 12 feet high along the length of the church.

After the construction of the new houses around Dower Road from 1955 onwards the church membership grew rapidly. During the 1950's and 60's as many as 70 young people met after Sunday evening worship for fellowship and 7 entered the Methodist ministry from Four Oaks Church, candidating from the Sutton Park Methodist Circuit.

Restoration and Extension

By the 1960's the stonework had deteriorated, needing heavy outlay in repair costs.

In 1969, a major extension scheme was carried out and the small hall, extra rooms, new toilets and kitchen were built.

In 1976, the church became a Grade 2 listed building, which may be regarded as prestigious but does create its own problems.

In 1986, more work was necessary to provide storage space, an accessible entry and toilets for the disabled and the upgrading of the kitchen.

1996 saw the refurbishment of the chancel area to enable us to have a more varied style of worship. The church received the gift of a new stained glass window at the rear of the church in memory of a past member.

The Centenary Appeal for £200,000 was for the replacement of the central heating, new lighting and re-wiring, new toilets, decorating and repairs to the tower stonework.

Multimedia equipment was purchased in 2002 to enable and provide greater flexibility and opportunity within worship for the present time and the future. New floodlighting was installed in 2003 our centenary year. During 2012 the kitchen was modernised to comply with current food hygiene regulations.

In the 21st century we are continuing to improve the premises and ensure that Four Oaks Methodist Church is a vibrant part of the local community.

Jim Hart

A SMALL PLACE ON LEYFIELDS

The Story Of A West Midlands 'Planting' 50 Years Ago

This article is dedicated to the memory of Lily Elsborg, one of three founder members of the school/church (my wife being one of the others), who is still known round the area as the 'brick lady' because of her great enthusiasm and hard work canvassing people to contribute to the fund that is mentioned in the article - even though it was so long ago. An amazing lady!

Since Methodism 'came indoors' as it were, its outward manifestations all seemed to be in the grand 19th Century tradition of church building, whether imposing structures in town centres or small village chapels. We all have experience of such places, with their hard pews, high ceilings, grand pulpits and ornate porticos. So to join a small fellowship in a 1950's junior school was a very new experience for those involved. Nowadays, it would be called a 'planting', although over 50 years ago that term was not current; rather it was a very tentative venture about which many in the local circuit were frankly very anxious.

So it was that in the early 1960s the Flaxhill Free Church began to meet in a school of that name in Tamworth, previously a small, ancient market town in Staffordshire but then on the cusp of great change.

In 1957, it had signed the first of several overspill agreements with Birmingham City Council, which led to the planning of the large Leyfields council estate on the northern edge of the town. Within this development the local council had reserved three sites for church buildings that were offered respectively to the Anglicans, the Catholic Church and the local Free Church Federal Council. The Catholics decided from the outset not to be involved, the Anglicans purchased one of the sites and moved rapidly to building, whilst the third site (costing £300) was considered for a short while by the Baptists. However, having carried out a year's mission during 1961 in the surrounding area they decided against going ahead and the task of establishing a presence was handed on to the Tamworth Methodist Circuit, which was thought to have a better chance of raising the money for the project through gifts and loans not available to other free church denominations. Thus the Flaxhill Free Church was established, drawing its fellowship from the few members of other churches in the circuit who were willing to be transferred. The process of firstly sustaining itself and secondly working towards its own building began. For several years, this infant fellowship struggled to survive but the faith and commitment of these first members kept it going and as the Leyfields estate began to rise on the fields earmarked for it, a few more people joined the little band. Interestingly although adults were few, the Sunday school grew rapidly as young families moved onto the estate and it soon had over 100 children attending regularly. Raising the funds for a new building was the central task of the fellowship as meeting in a school (and other venues such as local sports clubs) was never going to be a viable long-term option. Alongside all the customary methods such as jumble sales, summer and winter fayres, coffee mornings and barbeques the major source of revenue was the 'Buy A Brick' scheme whereby local residents agreed to donate a weekly amount, with each shilling they gave 'buying' a brick. Even so, without other sources of funding accumulating sufficient money for the project was going to take a long time. However, the circuit was successful in obtaining a number of gifts to supplement these local efforts, including £9,000 from the Joseph Rank Benevolent Trust and further help from the Chapel Department of the church.

Finally, the foundation stone of a single storey, rather utilitarian structure in the 60's idiom was laid in 1965, with the completed church being dedicated with great local ceremony in September 1966. Practical contributions by many local well-wishers, who gifted items such as the pulpit and communion rail to help furnish the interior, were of immense benefit, but it took several more years of fund-raising to pay off the outstanding debt on the construction, with the final cost of the building being £65,000. (In comparison new houses in the town at that time cost around £3,000 to £4,000.)

It is hard in some ways to capture or recall the atmosphere of that time. Once the new building was open – successively named Gillway Methodist Church and finally St. Andrew's – the congregation increased, young families appeared and a wide range of activities was initiated. At its highest, membership stood at 51. There was a thriving Sunday school and Guide and Scout groups for the young people, a women's fellowship, a young wives' group, a fellowship for the disabled, and a nursery group run as a commercial letting. In short, the kind of witness that had been prayed for long, hard years before. Now that St. Andrew's is moving towards its Golden Anniversary, a little retrospection is natural. As with a family, one can look back over the intervening years and see things in a wider perspective. The effect of wider social changes has not been in our favour. The population on the estate is now either old or very young and low paid employment is the norm in the area, if indeed one has a job, so life can be a struggle. Two parent families seem now more of an exception than the rule and petty crime and vandalism are constants. Added to these local factors the increasing secularisation of society tends to make church-going seem almost an oddity, militating against the shopping, sport and entertainment that constitute a Sunday for most people. A small fellowship is more 'at risk' in such a changed world, but the congregation at St. Andrew's, although fewer and older now, still bears witness in more modern ways. Around our fortieth year, it was felt the building itself was becoming no longer 'fit for purpose' and certainly did not meet modern needs and regulations, for example the lack of toilet facilities for the disabled. A major refurbishment generously funded by grants and loans from many sources including the local circuit helped create virtually a new interior (at something like three times the cost of the original building) and with it a new mood of optimism. The improvements have given us more financial security by generating a raft of weekday lettings by community groups but more importantly have enhanced our witness and outreach through such means as a Toddle-In group and Messy Church, a weekly project for vulnerable people that offers companionship, a simple meal and a prayer time, and a growing uniformed group embracing beavers, cubs and scouts. Forms of worship have changed as well to include monthly midweek communion, joint services with our neighbouring Anglican sisters and brothers down the road and the two other Methodist fellowships in the town, and a monthly 'all-age' service aimed at bringing back children and parents to the church. It would be dishonest to claim that all the changes described above have helped or benefited us. Like many other congregations we have mostly lost contact with the young, have an ageing profile and a small core of workers, and lack the sort of 'heritage' older churches might possess. Nonetheless, the flame of faith and witness still burns within us and its light shines around us for all to see if they care to look. 2016 will bring us to our fiftieth year in the hope that St. Andrew's, in whatever form, will continue for many more!

P. W. Rickwood

SPRINGDALE METHODIST CHURCH, PENN, WOLVERHAMPTON

From A Cinema To A Constantly Developing Church.

For the minister and leaders of the Beckminster Methodist Church in the leafy southern suburbs of Wolverhampton, mission was the life blood of their vision. The story of Springdale Methodist Church is a thrilling and inspiring story of God's people doggedly responding to an opportunity to spread the Gospel and serve the ever-growing suburb around Springhill and Warstones.

Services Begin At Springhill

The vision was caught and, with enthusiasm, the Rev. Arthur N. Rose M.A. and the leaders of Beckminster Methodist Church earmarked Springhill at the southern end of Warstones Road in Penn as being a good place to start a new Methodist church. Although no suitable land to build a church on had been identified, on 17th July 1936 the Springhill Methodist Church Trust was formed and a scheme outlined. The trustees looked at a number of possible sites. Eventually, a plot of land in Springhill

Lane was purchased on 3rd May 1937 at a cost of £492. On 26th November 1937, a building scheme for a church at a cost of £4,500 was approved. Soon, the Springhill Methodist Mission was started in two cottages. Mr Victor Cox started a Sunday school in his home at 292 Warstones Road, as well as a men's friendship circle.

At the Wolverhampton Trinity Circuit Local Preachers' Meeting on 31st May 1938, the new site was discussed. The meeting decided that, as a first step to starting a Methodist church in Penn, open-air services should be held on the newly acquired land in Springfield Lane. After visiting the site to see if holding an open-air service was viable on the new site, the Rev. Arthur N. Rose reported to the next meeting held on 7th September 1938 that it was not possible to hold open-air meetings on the Springhill site because of the condition of the ground. All was not lost when he reported that Mr John L. Cotterell had intimated that there was an opportunity to hold a service in the Penn cinema on Warstones Road.

Methodist Worship Services In The Cinema

Mr Harry Shawcross, the manager of the cinema, was approached and he generously agreed that services might be held in the cinema lounge which he offered free of charge. Mr Arthur Tilsley, Circuit Steward, made a folding rostrum which he gave to the new society and Mr & Mrs Fleet loaned an organ for the services. 60 folding chairs were purchased at 6/3d each but these soon became redundant and were sold to Beckminster church for 15 shillings each. The first service was held 18th September 1938 at 6.30pm when the Rev. Arthur N. Rose preached to a 'packed house'. So successful were the services that soon they had to be held in the main body of the cinema. This new mission society appeared on the Trinity Circuit plan as PENN CINEMA. Members of the local preachers' meeting were asked to note that the services at the Penn cinema were to be 'mission' services and that a direct homely message should be used. Sadly, in September 1940, because of war and blackout restrictions, the services had to end.

Postwar Schemes For A New Church

After the war the Springhill scheme was reconsidered. In 1945, Mr John L. Cotterell contacted Mr W. Moss of architects Crouch, Butler & Savage, Birmingham, who had since the beginning of the century built many iconic church and civic buildings in Birmingham and surrounding areas. Some of the Methodist churches the practice had designed were Hall Green, Birmingham (1924), Beckminster Methodist Church, Wolverhampton (1926), New Road Methodist Church, Stourbridge (1928), Warley Woods Methodist Church, Abbey Road, Bearwood (1928), and Erdington Methodist Church, Slade Road, (1931). Mr Moss met Mr Cotterell at Springhill and agreed to 'unofficially' draw up an outline scheme for a church on the site. On 16th May 1946, the County Borough of Wolverhampton informed the Springhill trust that they had designated a site in Warstones Drive near to the Penn cinema, for a church and advised them to buy it. On 11th November 1948, the Springhill trustees asked Mr Moss to draw up a scheme for a church on the Warstones Drive site. As a result of the council's suggestion there was held an historic meeting in the billiards room of Ash Hill House, Ash Hill, Compton, Wolverhampton. It was the home of Mrs Sylvia May Davis

Green, the widow of Mr Davis Green. Mrs Davis Green, on the death of her husband, Davis Green, and his brother, Walford Green, became the managing director and owner of Lockerbie & Wilkinson of Tipton, the manufacturer of 'penny in the slot' brass door locks and vending machines. The chairman of the meeting was the Superintendent, the Rev. Dr E. Douglas Bebb, who asked the Rev. Norman C. Parsons, the minister of Beckminster, for his comments on the suitability of the Springhill Lane and the Warstones Drive sites. Mr Parsons said that he doubted the wisdom of building on the Springhill Lane site now that the County Borough of Wolverhampton had offered the Warstones Drive site. These comments resulted in a very heated argument, which led to the proposal that there should be a church on both the Springhill Lane site and the Warstones Drive site a mile away. The meeting appointed Walter Thrift, James Warnock, Albert Walsh and John L.Cotterell and gave them the onerous task of finding a more suitable site somewhere between the Springhill Lane and Warstones Drive sites.

The Vision Frustrated

The four men identified a very suitable site of about 7000 square yards on the corner of Warstones Road and Wynchcombe Avenue. Their hopes were dashed when they discovered it had been bought by Holt's Brewery of Holt Street, Birmingham, with a view to building a pub on the land. Nevertheless, the four officers met the directors of the brewery who, having listened to the plan to build a church, agreed to sell the site to the trustees for £500 and also indemnified the trustees against any road or other charges that might be imposed by Wolverhampton Council. Once the land was purchased on 27th June 1951, the trustees were told by Wolverhampton Council that it was their intentions to put a compulsory purchase order on the site to build flats. One of the four, Albert Walsh, was the legal adviser to the Coal Board. The Coal Board was at the time prospecting for coal in the Penn area. Mr Walsh said that the report by the Coal Board would not be published for some time and that the coal seams were so deep in the area that they would not affect a church on the site. He further said that until the Coal Board findings were published, Wolverhampton Council could proceed with their plans to build the flats. Albert Walsh urged the trustees to put in an application to Wolverhampton Council for permission to build the church, which he said, the council would have difficulty in refusing. Permission was granted for a church to be built on the new site. Mr W. Moss was appointed as the architect. A. M. Griffiths & Sons Ltd. (a well known Methodist Wolverhampton family firm of builders) successfully tendered to build the church at a cost of £11,379. The contract was signed with the builders on 10th October 1952.

The Sunday School Venture

Before the church was built, a Sunday school was started in Warstones Primary School canteen and was staffed by members of the Beckminster Sunday school. The Sunday school opened on 15th June 1952, with 33 children and Geoffrey Race who, at the time of writing, regularly worships at Springdale Methodist Church, Margaret Race, Victor Cox, Doris Horobin, Colin Smith, Stanley Loweth and John L. Cotterell as the staff. By the end of the year there were 100 scholars on the register. On the opening day of the Sunday school the children and staff sang to a tape recorder and when the Rev. Norman C. Parsons told the

Beckminster congregation that evening that the Sunday school had started but they had no piano, one was gifted and was in use the following Sunday.

Stone Laying

On 28th March 1953, the stone laying ceremony was held at 3.00pm in the presence of the Mayor and Mayoress of Wolverhampton, Alderman and Mrs Harold T. Fullwood. The Chairman was Mr Albert Walsh M.B.E. LL.B. There were four stones laid, one by Mrs Sylvia May Davis Green. She had taken an active interest in the project and was a benefactor. Another stone was laid by Mr Albert Walsh M.B.E. LL.B whose legal skill and wise advice had made the scheme possible. The other two were laid by the superintendent minister of the Trinity Methodist Circuit, Rev. Dr E. Douglas Bebb, and the Rev. Norman C. Parsons, the minister of Beckminster and Springdale Methodist churches.

The Church Is Opened At Last

The long awaited church was designed as a multipurpose building, with removable fittings so that it could also be used for weekday activities and youth work. The building was a solid brick structure with no cavity walls. It had an entrance with steps but no handrail. There was a small foyer. Over the entrance was a gallery, which could only be accessed by a removable ladder. At the end of the church opposite the entrance was a stage. On the ground floor in front of the stage was a movable pulpit, communion rail and furniture. Heating was provided by overhead electric fires. The seating was wooden chairs. When the dual-purpose building was erected, it was envisaged that a large purpose-built church would at some future date be built alongside the first building.

The church opening ceremony for this building was held on Saturday 24th October 1953. The ceremony started at the entrance with the singing of the Doxology and the Lord's Prayer, followed by Mrs Sylvia May Davis Green, in the presence of the Mayor of Wolverhampton, Alderman Mrs Alice A. Braybrook (Wolverhampton's first woman mayor) and the Mayoress, formally unlocking the door and declaring the building open.

There followed a service conducted by the ministers of the Wolverhampton Trinity Methodist Circuit with the District Chairman, Rev. Leslie Davison B.D., preaching. The opening celebration continued at 7.00pm with a public meeting presided over by Mr Arthur Vernon.

On Sunday 25th October at 11.00am, Rev. Dr E. Douglas Bebb took the service. In the afternoon at 3.00pm the Sunday school children and the teachers walked in procession from Warstones Junior School to the new church where they were welcomed by the Rev. Norman C. Parsons and Deaconess Clare Powers. This was followed by a special Children's Service, which was led by the Rev. Norman C. Parsons. From then on, the Sunday school was held in the church at 3.00pm. The celebration continued at the evening service that was followed by the Sacrament of Holy Communion, led by Rev. Norman C. Parsons with Sister Clare Powers assisting. The first Sunday school anniversary was held in the church on 13th June 1954 at 3.00pm and was led by Mr Geoffrey Race with Mr Norman Griffiths playing the piano.

From Strength To Strength

The new church soon began to gather its congregation and membership, under the leadership of the minister and deaconess, from the newly built housing area of Penn. At the beginning, there was no organ to lead the singing but that deficiency was remedied when Mr George Stone donated a Compton organ that is now an exhibit in a museum. A choir was started. Within a year of the opening of the church, the Women's Fellowship started with 100 members and a men's meeting met weekly in the evenings. A few years later, a wives' group commenced with 30 members and the youth club was started. In 1954, the 21st Wolverhampton Scout Group was formed as was the Girl Guides company. These were followed by keep fit classes, a shell group, a play group, and a youth fellowship. With all these activities and their growing numbers attending the groups there was a need for larger premises. The first expansion was a wooden hut, but the need for a brick-built youth centre was obvious. In 1963, the Rev. Norman Peck promoted the idea of a permanent youth building and, following sponsored walks and a whole raft of fund raising activities and a generous donation from the Joseph Rank Trust, the new Youth and Community Centre was opened on November 18th 1967 by Mr George C. Stone. The chairman of the district, the Rev. Brian S. O'Gorman, dedicated the centre. Shortly after the opening of the centre, community groups started to use the centre one being the Multiple Sclerosis Society which still holds its weekly Day Centre on the premises.

21st Century Development Scheme

By 2000, the church building was in need of restoration and following a General Church Meeting and Church Council it was agreed to explore options for renovation. The Church Council appointed a working committee under the chairmanship of the Rev. Donald H. Ryan (Project Manager). Each member of the committee was appointed to a specific task. Mrs Lesley Cook, secretary, Mrs Nicola Jones, funds raiser, Mrs Barbara Morris, treasurer. Later the committee was strengthened when Mr Richard Gould joined the committee and became the joint project manager. The first aim of the project was to provide access for the disabled. Mr Ian Lewis of Lewis Architecture Ltd. was appointed as the architect and asked to devise a scheme to provide access and toilet facilities for the disabled.

To give access for the disabled meant major alterations to the church and extensive restoration. The need to be sensitive to the needs of the disabled meant that the church interior could be redesigned to meet modern forms of worship. The scheme with estimated costs was put to the Church Council. After much detailed discussion, the scheme was adopted as the 2003 - 50th anniversary year project. The scheme was designed to give access for people with different forms of disability, such as wheelchair users, people with poor eyesight, the deaf and the hard of hearing. This required removing the stepped entrance, gallery and foyer and making a new entrance at ground level. The church orientation was turned around which created a dedicated communion area. Included in the planned renovation was the lining of the inside of the solid brick walls with insulated plaster board, a new heating scheme, new modern chairs, new communion table, baptismal font and pulpit. During the restoration asbestos was discovered in the roof that led to an asbestos survey and its safe removal. The roof was then inspected and found to be in need of replacement immediately. Also included in the redevelopment were the restoration of the electronic organ and the provision of an electronic piano. When the work was completed the church was re-dedicated on 12th September 2014 in a service led by the minister Rev. Philip Summers and the Rev. Donald H. Ryan.

The Final Phase

The next phase was to raise money to build an atrium to link the church and the community centre with disabled access between the two buildings. As soon as the money was in hand the work was started. The design gave a light and airy welcoming glazed space with the added facility for a comfortably furnished warm entrance to the church and community centre. The ramp now gave people of all abilities easy access for the first time to move from the church to the community centre.

Two members of our church family who are well known professional artists in glass with an outstanding reputation, Allister and Teresa Malcolm, created and gifted three specially designed art works as their gift to the church.

50 Years of Methodist and Wesley Research

The new extension was dedicated at a service held on 16th October 2011, which was led by Rev. Donald H. Ryan and the Wolverhampton Circuit Superintendent, the Rev. David F. Lavender with the Wolverhampton & Shrewsbury District Chair, Rev. John D. Howard taking part. The minister, Rev. Dr Robert E. Ely, dedicated the atrium. At the service a specially written inspirational poem by Mrs Sheila Barnfather was read. The service was followed by the celebration reception and exhibition in the church hall and new atrium.

The cutting of the celebration cake by Mr Geoffrey Race and Mrs Freda Bristow, two of the founding members was a very poignant moment. The church and hall were full to overflowing with people, including some who had travelled long distances for this very special event in Springdale's ever-developing exciting story, mission and ministry.

Donald H. Ryan

ENGELBERG METHODIST MHA CARE HOME WOLVERHAMPTON

Golden Jubilee

The aptly named Methodist Care Home for the Aged, Engelberg – Angel Mountain, is on rising ground in Ash Hill, in the leafy suburbs of Wolverhampton. The residents are surrounded by loving, friendly care from trained professionals who enrich their lives with dignity, sensitivity, compassion and friendship.

On 21st April 2016, the home will celebrate its 50th anniversary. In 1965, the Wolverhampton & Shrewsbury Methodist District Chairman, Rev. Brian S. O'Gorman, identified the need for a Methodist care home for the elderly in or near Wolverhampton. He shared his vision with people in the area, and the Methodist businessman and founder of a footware business, Mr John A. Bates of Newbridge Crescent, Wolverhampton, responded. He offered a donation of £50,000 towards the cost of opening a MHA home in or near Wolverhampton. Mr Bates donated the money in memory of his wife, Blanche, who had died in 1963. The MHA raised another £40,000 to make the project viable.

A suitable private residence called Clareton with a large garden, located in Ash Hill, came onto the market and was bought by the Methodist Homes for the Aged. The house was converted and extended to accommodate 34 residents. In addition to single bedrooms, there were 6 double bed-sitting rooms, a dining room, a lounge, a quiet room, a tea bar, restrooms and a dispensary for the use of doctors and a chiropodist. On the 17th February 1966, it was registered by Staffordshire County Council under Section 37 of The National Assistance Act 1948, as a Home for Old Persons.

On 21st April 1966, Mr John A. Bates officially opened the home. In his opening speech he said, "This is a home for old people – a perfect home – a home that is exactly as a home means to you and me – a place of joy, and a place of hope and happiness." The home was given the name Engelberg as a reminder of the place in Switzerland where John and Blanche found great happiness on their honeymoon. Speaking of his wife, Mr Bates said, "She had a sweet life, well lived, and today she is remembered with gratitude."

The Chairman of the General Committee of the Methodist Homes of the Aged, Sir George William Martin, reminded the people that his father, Rev. Edward Martin, was the Superintendent Minister of the Darlington Street Wesleyan Circuit, Wolverhampton, from 1908 to 1911 and minister of the newly built 1901 church which was the most significant and architecturally impressive domed building in the town. He also spoke of the generosity of the Methodist people. Mr G. V. Norman Bates, the son of the benefactor, chaired the opening dedication ceremony. He reminded the assembly that the date was the 21st, which was a significant date and number. It was the

Queen's birthday. It was the 21st Anniversary of the Methodist Homes for the Aged and Engelberg was the 21st home the MHA had established.

The Inspired Vision

By the 1930's, the century-old Poor Law Report (1834) 'workhouse test', which separated the deserving poor from the undeserving poor, was ended. Depending on how you read history, the workhouse system finished in 1930 although many claim that it did not end until the National Health Service was implemented in 1948. In 1930, the Board of Guardians was abolished. Many of the workhouses were renamed Public Assistance Institutions and their responsibility and financial support fell to local councils. In 1948, many of the buildings, which had been workhouses, became hospital buildings, as is the case in Wolverhampton. In 1903, the Wolverhampton workhouse was relocated to a new building to house around 700 poor people with an adjoining infirmary for around 375 sick. The present modern New Cross Hospital is now on the site, where there are still remnants of the old building. The vision that became the Methodist Homes for the Aged was the inspired vision of the Rev. Walter Hall (1876-1966). In 1935, Walter Hall saw that there was a need to provide safe and secure homes for the care for older people. His vision was to have a comfortable residential home from home. Walter Hall was a minister of the United Methodist Church until the 1932 Act of Union, which formed the Methodist Church of Great Britain. He had served in Jamaica and then in several English circuits. He became the secretary of the North London Methodist District and then became its chairman. After 40 years ministry, he became a supernumerary minister in 1945. He did not 'sit down' in the Tottenham Circuit. It was said in his official *Minutes of the Methodist Conference Obituary* that his most active work was done in his retirement years. It was in the later years of his busy ministry and the opening years of his retirement that he had the vision and sense of urgency that the Methodist Church should open a home for the elderly.

The First Tentative Steps

In 1935, Lord Rank (1854-1943) received a letter from Walter Hall saying that the former United Methodist deaconess hostel, Bowran House, in Battersea, was on the market and could be purchased for £2500. He included the architect's plans and said that with an extension it could accommodate about 10 residents and staff. He courteously asked if Lord Rank, from his charitable fund, would consider buying it. He also wrote to Rev. C. Ensor Walters (1872-1938), who regularly met with Lord Rank to discuss requests for charity gifts. There was no response from Lord Rank. Sometime later, Mr Hall met a 65 year old lady (who was looking 10 years older), who told him that she had to leave her home because she did not have enough money for the rent. She pleaded with him, "Please, Mr Hall, don't let them take me to the Union!" (a term often used for the workhouse). In 1942, he spoke to a number of eminent Methodist people who supported his vision. Despite the restrictions and limitations that WW2 put on all projects because of the demands to use all available resources to fight the war, Walter Hall continued to advocate the need for a home for the elderly.

A Methodist Home For The Elderly Takes Root

Walter Hall brought to the Methodist Conference in 1943, which was meeting in Birmingham, the revolutionary and far-seeing proposal that the Methodist Church should establish residential homes for older people. The idea was not novel but it was new to the Methodist Conference. At the time, there were already a number of residential homes in existence run by other Christian denominations and charities, some with very restrictive regulations and little personal privacy. After much debate, the Methodist Conference gave its approval to the idea of establishing residential homes for older people based on the Christian principles of love, compassion and respect. At the time, many of the poorer people were housed in workhouses. In 1943, Lord Rank died but he had had the foresight to set up a charity to distribute the funds he had placed in the Joseph Rank Benevolent Trust.

The Seal Of Approval

A committee was set up by the Methodist Conference and in their report to the Conference they said that consideration should be given to the provision of Methodist homes providing 'maximum privacy, and economic independence, combined with common meals and fellowship' for people aged 60 and above. The 1944 Methodist Conference approved the name 'Methodist Homes for the Aged' and set up a conference committee with Walter Hall, several Methodist ministers, and 15 laymen, including Lord Rochester (1876-1955) (H.M. Paymaster General and Vice President of the Methodist Conference 1941), and Sir George William Martin, who became the first chairman of MHA

(Lord Mayor of Leeds 1946 and a future High Sheriff of Yorkshire), a 'son of the manse'. With this seal of approval the committee pursued the project. Despite looking after his ailing wife, Walter remained very committed to the scheme. Funds were scarce so he employed a temporary typist 3 days a week, using his study as the office to make the scheme become a reality. In 1945, Rylands at Wallington, Surrey was opened. It provided accommodation for 12 elderly ladies.

The Increasing Need Is Faced With Confidence

In the first 30 years, an average of one new MHA home was opened. From 1956, there was a preference for purpose built homes. From 1975, until 1996 the MHA operated under the umbrella of the Methodist Conference Division of Social Responsibility, but was always a separate charity with a separate Board of Trustees. During the time of Davis L. Wigley as the Chief Executive (1982-1997), the residential care facilities progressed; developed schemes of sheltered housing, dementia care and community based 'Live at Home' schemes were started.

The Challenge Of The Changing Requirements Of Society Is Faced.

The MHA has from the beginning expanded its work to meet emerging community needs. In 1977, it offered sheltered accommodation for rent. In 1988, the first 'Live at Home' project was set up to provide support by trained volunteers, which made it possible for older people to continue to live in their own homes. In 1989, the first specialist nursing care home was built. With the growing situation of older people suffering from dementia, in 1997 MHA offered care in a purpose built care home which met their special medical, social and spiritual needs. This was further developed in 2004, with a scheme to support dementia care to people living in their own homes. The needs of people with dementia was further met when the MHA employed, in 2008, its first in-house Music Therapist which has been a valued development and has been further developed by a grant from the Big Lottery Teaching Community Fund. At the time of writing, a new imaginative development has been opened at Southport to provide a supportive environment and housing for couples where one partner has dementia. There is specialist support on site during the day and night.

In 2007, the MHA introduced training to its staff so that they could become qualified in reflexology, which has enhanced the care and well being of residents.

A very exciting and new scheme came into being in 2009, when the MHA acquired the retirement village Auchlochan, in Lanarkshire. Scotland.

The MHA Receives Prestigious Recognition

The outstanding quality of the MHA standards of care was recognised 2012, when, with honour, it received recognition as the Best Residential Care Provider at the Laing & Buisson Independent Healthcare Awards.

In the same year, in recognition of valuable and dedicated service of the vast number of volunteers, it was awarded the Queen's Diamond Jubilee Volunteering Award.

Spiritual Needs Addressed

With its foundation rooted in the Methodist denomination, all its schemes have been, and are, open to both Methodists and friends of other denominations, as well as those with no religious affiliation. The MHA projects have an appointed chaplain. Some are Methodist, others are members of other denominations. Some are presbyters, other are not, but all are dedicated to giving the people in their oversight personal as well as collective spiritual support. The chaplains also give valued support to members of the staff.

Today And The Future

The MHA is currently the second largest provider of specialist services for the elderly in the not-for-profit sector, serving about 16,000 people.

In the spirit of the way that the founder and pioneers of the MHA set out to offer a better choice for older people to live in a better environment with care and security, so the present MHA is expanding and developing its choice of person-centred care in an ever changing environment. Residential homes still are a very special need met by MHA, along with all its other visionary projects. MHA is monitoring the new needs of the elderly and are constantly looking at and planning how best they can be met.

MHA fosters care, compassion and respect for individual spiritual needs. Whilst our work is inspired by the Christian faith, we have always welcomed people from all religious traditions, as well as those without any religious affiliation. Every MHA care service is supported by a dedicated chaplain, who may come from a range of denominations. Some are ordained ministers and others are lay people. They provide a listening presence and one-to-one pastoral support for all residents and staff members, whatever their backgrounds or need, and organise worship for those who wish to participate. Where appropriate, residents are encouraged to maintain links with local faith communities.

For many residents in our care homes, MHA will provide them with their last home. Our chaplains have a particular role in helping residents and their relatives approach their final years, hopefully with a sense of acceptance, peace and fulfilment. In all of its services the MHA continues, through the high standards of professionalism of its carers and staff, to give each individual compassionate care. The carers seek to nurture each person's body, mind and spirit, so bringing a good quality of meaning and purpose in life to all who are cared for.

In the West Midlands there are MHA care homes at:
    Cedar Lodge, Bearley Cross, Warwickshire
    Herondale, Birmingham
    Kingfisher, Birmingham
    Abbey Park, Coventry
    Allesley Hall, Coventry
    Charnwood House, Coventry
    Homewood, Leamington Spa, Warwickshire
    Cedar Lawn, Stratford upon Avon
    Weston Queensway, Stafford
    Briar Hill House, Rugeley
    Engelberg, Wolverhampton
    Waterside, Wednesfield, Wolverhampton

There are MHA Housing Schemes at:
  The Dovecotes, Coventry
  Aldersgate, Nuneaton
  Bridgecourt, Wednesfield, Wolverhampton

Donald H. Ryan

OBSERVING METHODIST WORSHIP: WORCESTER, 1940 AND 1973

Much Methodist history is written from Methodism's own archival sources, but valuable insights can also be gained from external views. Participant observation is a longstanding journalistic, anthropological, and sociological technique whereby observers from outside the community being studied participate in its activities and record their findings. This essay transcribes two such observer reports of public worship in the same Methodist church in 1940 and 1973.

The church concerned is Pump Street, Worcester, of Wesleyan heritage. It opened in 1796 and was replaced in 1813, 1902 (with seating for 727 by 1940), and 1968 (when it was designated St Andrew's Church, with a capacity of 326). The church's history is told in Helen Ladd's *Two Saints in Pump Street: 200 Years of Methodism in Worcester, 1796-1996* (1996).

The first observation was made in 1940 by John Alfred Atkins (1916-2009), known as Jack, who had graduated in History from Bristol University in 1938 and later became a writer and teacher (see obituary in *The Guardian*, 18 May 2009). Between June and November 1940, he and his new wife were based in Worcester as a two-person research outpost of Mass

Observation (MO), created in 1937 to investigate the anthropology of everyday life. They wrote up their findings in MO File Report 475, preserved at the MO Archive, The Keep, Brighton (SxMOA1/1/5/10/36), together with the raw materials for the study (principally at SxMOA1/2/66/21).

Jack Atkins made a dozen or so observations of church services in Worcester during summer 1940 (SxMOA1/2/47/1/D/1, SxMOA1/2/66/21/A/5), two of which were Methodist. One was of evening worship (then still the principal Sunday service) at Pump Street on 4th August, reproduced here with permission of Curtis Brown Group Ltd., London on behalf of the trustees of the Mass Observation Archive. A few editorial annotations appear within square brackets. Atkins did not mention the name of the minister taking the service, but the three non-supernumerary ministers in the Worcester Circuit that year were William Clifford Caddy (1885-1967), superintendent, Harold Dunn Wilson (1893-1969), and Jeffrey Spencer (1912-2000).

Another observation was made of a morning service (the principal one on Sunday by that time) by the present writer in 1973, when he was a 23-year-old doctoral student at Oxford. He was staying with some Methodist acquaintances, the Hewitts, near Pershore for the weekend and accompanied them to the service at Pump Street, where they worshipped. He was experimenting with several methodologies for researching the history of Methodism and this was his first formal attempt at participant observation.

The 1973 service was taken by Derrick Amphlet Greeves (1913-91), superintendent minister of the Worcester Circuit (see obituaries in *The Times*, 20 March 1991; *Methodist*

Recorder, 28 March 1991; and *Minutes of Conference*, 1991, pp. 40-1). A broadcaster and author, the high point of his ministry was his succession in 1955 of William Sangster as superintendent of Westminster Central Hall, where Greeves stayed for nine years.

4th August 1940, 6.30pm, Minister Unspecified, Observed By Jack Atkins

There were nearly 150 people present, the church being fairly full. The choir was 20 strong, 15 of these being women. A gallery ran all the way round three walls, but the part [the] observer could see was practically empty. The congregation was mostly female, although not heavily so. There was also a fairly high percentage of young men present.

Hymns etc.

678	'Lord of the worlds above'
167	'Fierce raged the tempest o'er the deep'
528	'In heavenly love abiding'
615	'Guide me, o thou great Jehovah'
490	'Fight the good fight with all thy might'

The preacher read Psalm 86.

Prayers

The prayers had very little connection with a war situation. The general theme was that God should teach us to lead good lives and that He should do the same for the nation as a whole. After this the minister prayed for the lads in the King's forces and those who minister unto them.

Sermon

The preacher had been visiting a sick friend during the week and this friend had shown him a book he had just finished reading. It was on Billy Sunday, the great American baseball player who had been converted to Christ. He said he had read a book on Billy Sunday, but not this particular one, so his friend invited him to read it. He took it home and once again was impressed by the story of Billy Sunday.

As a young fellow of twenty, he had been playing baseball for his local White Socks team when the representative of a big championship team saw him, was impressed, and went up to Billy and asked him if he would like to join the championship side. A few weeks later, Billy was in their first team, making big money. One afternoon he came out of a saloon with some other members of the side – it was a Sunday afternoon – and, it being very hot, they all sat down on the kerb. At that moment, a little mission band came down the road and started playing. After listening for a few minutes, Billy couldn't stand it any longer – they were singing the very hymns his mother had taught him as a child – and he got up and said, "I'm through, fellows – I'm going to Christ!" and he walked away and joined the band. Next day when he got to the training ground he told them that he meant it, that he was really going to give himself to Christ.

Many people have criticised Sunday for his unorthodox methods but as [John Raleigh] Mott says, it is impossible to fool a large body of students. The students of all the American universities believed in Sunday; they know if a man is sincere, and if he is insincere they also know it. When Sunday was converted he thought to himself, "I wonder what will become of the other fellows who were sitting on that kerb? What became of them?"

There was Mike Kelly, being paid 4,700 dollars a week. What became of him? When he died, he didn't even leave enough to pay his funeral expenses. There was Ed Williamson. What became of him? He came to this country on an exhibition tour. On the way back to America there was a tremendous storm and, believing his end was near, he went down on his knees and prayed to God to spare him and he would become a Christian. He was spared, but when he got home did he become a Christian? He forgot all about it. He died a drunkard. Then there was Frank Flynn — what of him? When he lay on his deathbed he was frightened and he sent for Sunday and asked him to offer up a prayer for him. He had been a fine player of games but who won the Game of Life? Billy Sunday.

When I had read his story again, I began to think of the passages in the Bible where games are mentioned. St Paul mentioned a race and the writer of the Epistle to the Hebrews does likewise. They probably had the Olympic Games in mind. Life is a contest. The same thought occurred to Sir Ernest Shackleton when he said, "Life is a game, but it is not a trivial game." Exactly — it is the biggest game of all. What do we mean by a game, a contest? We usually imply the sense of struggle and it is the same in life. We all try to win, to register a success.

Having reached this point, I took down from my shelf some of my books and began to look at those that gave hints for making a success of things. They all gave the same advice, especially for young people. The qualities required were courage, patience, unselfishness, character – yes, they all said character – personality, perseverance, thoughtfulness – yes, thoughtfulness. Everyone is born into this world for some purpose and it is his duty to discover this purpose and then make a success of it.

There is a story about Will McLaughlin going into his uncle's room when he was preparing one of his sermons. Will asked him what he was doing, and his famous uncle [Frank Gunsaulus] said he was compiling a sermon on the text "for what purpose was I born unto this hour?" [John 18:37]. Will, that splendid young fellow, athlete and great student, laughed and said, "I don't know why I was born unto this hour." Then he went out and began to walk down the street. He was passing a theatre where his uncle was going to preach the next week when he heard a woman shout, "Fire!" he dashed into the theatre, put a plank out of the window and managed to save 17 women. He had just got the seventeenth out when the plank broke and crashed to the ground. He was carried to the hospital, severely burned, and the doctor who examined him said he could not live. His uncle was sent for and when he arrived Will said, "I know for what purpose I was born unto this hour."

A few weeks later some American businessmen and English businessmen met in a hotel, in gay Paris, as it used to be called. One of them had also been in that fire and he told the others that he had fought like a devil to escape. Fought like a devil to save his own worthless life, while Will McLaughlin had saved the lives of 17 women! Which of those two won the Game of Life? We hear a lot of talk nowadays, saying we can't win and such things as that. But we can if we find out what is our purpose and apply ourselves to it in the way Will McLaughlin did when he realised his own purpose.

Announcements

Wednesday afternoons, 3-3.20pm, short intercession services.

Anyone requiring information about the envelope system can get it from Mrs Godridge, Mr Osborn or the minister himself, or any of the stewards.

August 22nd, a church tea.

First Wednesday in September, women's missionary meeting.

Third Monday in September in the evening, Harvest Festival meeting.

House to house collections for hospital. There is no Daisy Day [fundraising event] in Worcester, hence it is impossible to raise great sums like they do in Birmingham, but instead a house to house collection has been arranged. So far only one person has volunteered. Last year the centre of the city was not collected from for the same reason, so it is hoped it will not occur again this year. Volunteers are asked to come forward, even if they could only do half a street.

Note
The choir also sang an anthem, 'Come, thou fount of every blessing'.

2nd September 1973, 10.45am, Minister Derrick Greeves. Observed By Clive Field

When we arrived at 10.15, 30 minutes before the service began, there were only two women sitting in the church [on the second floor] apart from the chapel stewards, busy both inside and out. The congregation began to arrive mostly after 10.35 and there were quite a few stragglers (about three or four families, possibly 20 persons in all) who arrived in the five minutes after the service began.

Total attendance was 67 men (but this includes the stewards), 77 women and 25 children (mainly young, under 10 years) plus the minister. The congregation was not so imbalanced as congregations elsewhere but the bulk of it was middle aged and elderly. There were not many young people and hardly any young people on their own. Indeed, most of the adult congregation was in pairs of men and women and there were few women who came alone. The social status of the congregation proved hard to ascertain but seemed very 'respectable'. Not all the men wore suits.

According to Mr Hewitt, the morning congregation was a little below usual, it still being holiday time and there being especially slightly fewer children than usual.

Both before and after the service, the congregation chatted in church, but not always quietly, and seemingly not on religious matters. It was generally attentive during the service itself. This began promptly at 10.45 and lasted 1 hour and 8 minutes. This was longer than the usual length, which was 1 hour almost exactly. The normal organist was not present and the substitute played his music rather slowly so that the singing got out of step somewhat, some singing faster than others. There was also a confirmation service for three new church members that lasted just over 10 minutes.

The order of service was as per the attached sheet [see over] but the last hymn was not sung. The call to worship consisted of two sentences only and the first prayer was also very brief. Immediately before the children left, the minister gave a short 3-4 minute children's 'address' on the subject of going back to school, urging them to befriend all strangers who were starting in different forms and schools. Since 10 at least of the children were under 5 years and many of the rest not much older, the address seemed to be irrelevant for some.

The second set of prayers was longer than the first but not half as long as the remarks the minister prefaced to them. His two themes were: a) the violence in the world, which is everywhere and no one is immune (when he lived in Chelsea he noted how robberies and violence were not only confined to inner London but also to very respectable suburbs) and b) the beginning of the new Methodist year. He called for good attendance at the circuit gathering at St Andrew's on Thursday night to welcome the two new ministers [Paul Hardy and Mark Davies]. He referred to the very poor turnout at Droitwich the day before to welcome the two. He thought this poor attendance might have been related to the showing of the Gillette cricket final on television or to people watching football and stressed, "it is not good enough, it is not good enough." He urged the congregation 'very pressingly' to come on Thursday. He said he was applying 'a three-line whip'. Ministers may not be angels with magic but they were proclaimers of a new Word.

His sermon lasted 13 minutes and was delivered with the aid of notes. He began by a reference to the three young adults awaiting confirmation and his theme was 'live, let live, and help live'. To live was not just to fill the day with amusement and good food. It was to live life to the fullest and to serve Christ in all one did. To let live was to be considerate to others and in particular to tolerate diversity of opinion in the church. He illustrated this by a story (evidently told before to some people present) about a Scotsman on a visit to England. On returning home the Scotsman related how funny the English were and told how one night at 2:00am a woman persisted in knocking on his window pane. When asked what the Scotsman did then, he replied that he continued to play his bagpipes. This brought a general outbreak of laughter from the congregation, as it was intended to do. To help live was to help give life to others (as, for example, by blood transfusions). The quality of the sermon was probably average but certainly not very inspiring. It was rather anecdotal and only for one very brief moment was Christ brought in – otherwise, it was entirely ethical.

The confirmation service was from the *Book of Offices* and consisted of most of the members' admission service and extracts from the Holy Communion service. The whole was performed as in prayer with congregational responses. As for the second prayer, but not for the first, some of the men knelt in prayer but very few, all the women sitting. The minister read the service in a sometimes mechanical fashion. Each of the new members was presented with a hymn book, *Book of Offices* or some such thing. Then they and the families received Communion. The Holy Communion service included the reading of the hymn and had its own benediction, so there was no general benediction at the end of the service.

The minister greeted all as they left and a majority of the congregation (though not all – possibly two-thirds) stopped for coffee afterwards in the hall [on the first floor]. The talk between adults was mainly social and the children were playing with cars, etc.

Order Of Service

Organ – two improvisations on Anglican chants, Dr A. Vernon Butcher

Call to worship

Hymn 669 (tune Repton, *Hymns and Songs*, 22)

Prayer and Lord's Prayer

Old Testament reading – Joshua 1:1-9

Hymn, verses 1 (*Methodist Hymn Book*, page 388)

The children leave

New Testament readings – Romans 12:1-5, Mark 1:14-20

Prayers

Offering and dedication

Hymn 719

Sermon

Hymn 431 (tune 183)

Confirmation in church membership – Joy Bonham, Susan Graham, Paul Griffin

The new members, with their family, will receive Holy Communion

Hymn 594

Blessing

Organ – Introduction and Fugue in E Flat, Dr A. Vernon Butcher

Clive D. Field

FRANCIS ASBURY: BLACK COUNTRY BOY TO AMERICA PIONEER

Family Fun Day Celebrating Asbury's 200th Anniversary at the Black Country Living Museum, 9 April 2016

Francis Asbury was the foremost pioneer bishop of Methodism in America. Dr Leonard Woolsey Bacon, in a volume of his *History of American Christianity*, says of Francis Asbury, "Very great is the debt that American Christianity owes to Francis Asbury. It may reasonably be doubted whether any one man, from the founding of the church in America until now, has achieved so much in the visible and traceable results of his work."

This remarkable pioneer was Francis Asbury who was born in Hampstead Bridge, Handsworth, Staffordshire around 20th August 1745. His parents were Joseph (1714-1798) and Elizabeth, née Rogers (?-1802). His father was a jobbing farmer and gardener to the Wyrleys of Hamstead Hall and the Goughs of Perry Hall. Joseph and Elizabeth were married in their local parish church, St Giles, Sheldon, South Birmingham, on 30th May 1742. They had a daughter, Sarah, (1743-1748) who was baptised at St Mary's Handsworth on 3rd May 1743. Both parents were Methodists. Because of family circumstances, Francis received a limited education. Asbury moved with his parents to a house in Newton Road, Great Barr, which today is preserved in his memory and may, by appointment, be visited. At an early age Francis became an apprentice chapemaker to John Griffin. (A chape was a decorative metal protective attachment to the bottom of a scabbard or sheath of a sword or dagger. It was also a metal decorative attachment which fixed the scabbard to a waist belt or a buckle to a belt.)

The young Asbury went with his deeply committed Christian mother to hear Alexander Mather, one of John Wesley's preachers, at Wednesbury. Mather recognised Asbury's deeply and remarkable spiritual commitment and cultivated it. Asbury was converted when he was 16. Just one year later, Mather authorised him to form and lead a 'Society class'. When Francis was eighteen, Mather appointed him a local preacher. His first sermon was in Manswood Cottage, near to the large farm house called The Manswood. Soon, with zeal, enthusiasm and a deep conviction that he had to advocate the Gospel of Jesus Christ, Asbury preached in the counties of Stafford, Warwick, Worcester and Derby. Also as we see in the chapter on the Four Oaks Methodist Church above Asbury regularly preached in the home of his close friend, Edward Hand. This was in Blake Street, Sutton Coldfield and was twice set on fire by those opposed to Methodist worship. Edward Hand was himself persecuted for his Methodist leanings and for allowing his home to be a Methodist preaching place. Asbury became one of Mr Wesley's preachers and entered the itinerancy in 1766 serving in the Bedfordshire, Colchester and Wiltshire Circuits,

It was with his friend Edward that Francis Asbury in 1771 spent his last evening in 'spiritual fellowship' before returning to his parents' home where he preached his final sermon in his homeland before leaving England to start his pioneer work in America. Asbury was never to return to England. His parents allowed their home to be a Methodist preaching house for more than 50 years and, when in old age and in financial straitened circumstances, Frances Asbury sent from his meagre stipend money to help them retain their home and to support the Methodist cause they led there.

Bishop Francis Asbury's Boyhood Home

The cottage is preserved as an historical site and is now called 'Bishop Asbury Cottage'. It is on its original site in Great Barr and in the care of the Sandwell Metropolitan Borough Council. It is not open except by appointment for groups. Individuals may visit on special open days. Information may be had from the Wednesbury Museum or on the Sandwell Metropolitan Council website.

In the Wesley Historical Society Proceedings Volume 32 page 83, J. M. Day records how the cottage was secured as an important historic building.

West Bromwich Council Receives A Letter

A letter from the International Methodist Historical Society dated 10th January 1950, was sent to West Bromwich Council. The letter pointed out that the cottage was the most important Methodist site in the Black Country and it would attract American visitors. The letter goes on to say that if it was to come on to the property market, it could be bought, preserved and furnished.

The Town Council's Response

In February 1950 the serving Mayor, Alderman Mrs Grace Wilkes J.P. and the Town Clerk met the Joint Managing Directors of the Darby Brewery Ltd., owners of the cottage. The Directors were already aware of the importance of the cottage and, with the efforts of their father, the late George Darby, the premises had been kept in good repair. Following the meeting, the council decided to start negotiations to purchase the cottage and its neighbouring property, Malt Shovel Cottage. The cottages were transferred to the Council on 6th April 1955.

The 'Listing'

West Bromwich Council, being aware of the historic significance of the cottage, earmarked it in 1949 for inclusion in the list submitted for listing. The building was eventually listed on 23rd September 1955.

The Next Chapter

At the time the cottage was the home of Mrs Randles and her family. She very kindly allowed American visitors into her home to view the premises, even though it was sometimes inconvenient. Mrs Randles, with good grace, showed the visitors around her home for which she received many tributes and words of appreciation. Regularly in the summer season Americans came knocking on her door to see this place that was so very important in their Methodist heritage and history. Mrs Randles moved in 1957 to another house close by.

From the time of the purchase of the premises, the Council Town Planning Committee liaised with the World Methodist Council through Rev. Dr Benson Perkins. Mr Thomas Rayson, the architect who had overseen the restoration of the Epworth Old Rectory, wrote a detailed report on the cottage. The World Methodist Council intimated that financial support might be available through them to renovate the property.

The two-storied brick-built property with two dormer windows under a tiled roof was restored and furnished with furniture from the historic period when the Asburys lived in the cottage. The property is on Newton Road, (next to The Malt Shovel), Great Barr, Sandwell, B43 6HN. On the cottage is a plaque which reads:

THIS COTTAGE
NOW THE PROPERTY OF THE
COUNTY BOROUGH OF WEST BROMWICH
WAS THE BOYHOOD HOME OF
FRANCIS ASBURY (1745 - 1816)
'THE PROPHET OF THE LONG ROAD'
WHO WAS SENT TO AMERICA BY JOHN WESLEY
IN 1771
AND BECAME THE FIRST BISHOP OF THE
AMERICAN METHODIST CHURCH
DEDICATED TO PERPETUAL REMEMBRANCE
IN ASSOCIATION WITH THE
WORLD METHODIST COUNCIL
AFTER RESTORATION
27th NOVEMBER 1959

During 2016, there will be held in the United Kingdom and the United States of America anniversary celebrations and projects to celebrate the life and ministry of Bishop Francis Asbury. In the United Kingdom, the Methodist Connexion 200th Anniversary Launch Event will be held at the Black Country Living Museum on Saturday 9th April.

Donald H. Ryan

BERTIE BISSELL (1902-1998)

A Godly man of prayer, leadership and peace

Baptised Bertie Bissell but better known as Bert Bissell, he was born in Goole, Yorkshire on 9th January 1902 and died on 2nd November 1998. At his own request, he was buried in the Glen Nevis Cemetery, Fort William. His parents were Joseph Benjamin Bissell (1868-1931) and Charlotte Elizabeth Bissell, née Allen, (1875-1954). Bert's parents were married in the summer of 1894 at Burslem, Staffordshire. They had five sons: Sidney (1897-1983), Horace (1900-1978), Bertie (1902-1998), Ewart (1911-1984), Ernest Roland (1914-1957), and a daughter who died in infancy. Joseph Bissell was an important Primitive Methodist minister who spent part of his ministry in the West Midlands, notably in Darlaston and Quinton, where he was the chaplain to the Bourne College staff and students, Coventry, Brierley Hill and Dudley.

Bert Bissell came with his family to Darlaston when he was 7 and remained in the West Midlands for the rest of his life. In 1915, his father was appointed to the Coventry Primitive Methodist Circuit. Bert, aged 13, took the entrance examination for the famous Coventry Bablake School. He passed and was given a scholarship place. The school is one of the oldest schools in the country, having been being founded in 1344 by Queen Isabella, Edward II's widow. At the age of 13, he was 'the new boy' in the school. His age contemporaries had been at the school for at least 2 years and were well established in their friendships with other boys. When the music master played some notes he asked Bert what they were and Bert replied, "I haven't the faintest idea." The music master responded by saying, "You're no good for the choir." That rather pleased Bert. He fared better when asked, "Can you play football?" His prowess as a footballer soon made him popular and accepted by the other boys. Bert was soon in the first eleven. He won a second scholarship at the school, which allowed him to become a boarder. He was also a good cricketer and played for the school team. When he became a boarder, he was asked to form a boarders' cricket team. None of the other boarders played cricket, so Bert got the sleepy and reluctant boys up daily at 6:00am for cricket practice. Under his charismatic leadership and training, the 'inner boys' beat the well-established school team. His single-mindedness in training the cricket team was a mark of the man in his mature years.

During this time he honed the skills that were to be the trademark in his future career as a leader of boys and men. His first training in public speaking was in the school Debating Society. Whilst being 'Head Prefect Indoors' he developed his pastoral skills as he sympathetically listened to the boys when they told him their troubles.

Following a bout of influenza which swept across Europe in 1918, and the prolonged illness that kept him at home, Bert left Bablake School and became a young entrepreneur selling clothing and shoes. The staff, parents of children at Bablake School and others gave him orders, which sustained and developed his business.

Even though Bert had left the school for years to come he was a regular and very welcome visitor to the prize days, school concerts and other events. Bert always gave warm and genuine encouragement to the boys whatever their ability. He applauded them on their academic successes and fine performances at the concerts.

Bert started a youth club in the Coventry Temperance Hall, which he called 'The League of Youth'. He invited speakers who were sportsmen. Footballers, cricketers and boxers were amongst the most popular to talk to the boys. Bert saw this club as a midway youth club for the boys from the Bablake School and as a way of introducing them to his 'Young Men's Class' which met at Vickers Street Methodist Church. Dudley

Bert Bissell's natural and skilful pastoral friendliness and his genuine warmth made him a welcome visitor to any home, even to houses where he was not known. This ability was a mark of his character, the key to his success. He could open easily and naturally a dialogue with people he had never met before, as well as being able to sustain a conversation with people who found it difficult to talk freely. Always in a hurry to see someone or to go to a meeting never meant that he did not have time to stop and talk to friend and stranger alike.

1933 was a major turning point in Bert's professional life when he joined the Dudley Magistrates Court to succeed the retiring Police Court Missionary. Bert became the first and tireless full-time Dudley Probation Officer. His skill in 'befriending' young people and others was a skill that other academics were to discover years after Bert had pioneered and developed this highly successful way of helping people. He was the person who developed and shaped the Probation Service in the Dudley area. He remained in post as Principal Probation Officer until he retired at the age of 65 some 34 years later. During these working years, his pastoral caring and genuine friendship helped many young people to turn around their lives by making them have confidence in themselves. He showed people they were valued members of the community. In 1959, Bert was awarded the M.B.E. for 25 years' service to the Probation Service.

Bert's father became the minister of Vicar Street Primitive Methodist Church in 1925. The church had been built in 1902 and was replaced in 1942 at a cost of £2,000. Vicar Street Church had the distinction of being the only Methodist Church that the government allowed to be built during the war years.

On 13th September 1925 Bert founded the Vicar Street Young Men's Bible Class with Jack and Denis Bloomer, Fred Preece and Bert Bache being the first members. The class later became affectionately known as the YMBC. Bert was to lead the class for over 70 years. At its peak in the 1930's, the YMBC had a membership of around 300. In 1931, Bert was appointed to be Lay Pastor of Vicar Street Chapel. Through his work as a probation officer many young men and ex-prisoners on licence found a haven in the Bible Class. During his time as leader, Bert, always the evangelical, brought many men to faith by inspired preaching, well informed knowledge of the Bible, leadership and genuine one-to-one conversations. Some 18 members of the YMBC later became ordained Christian ministers, most becoming Methodist Presbyters. Up to 100 became local preachers and many were appointed as class leaders.

From his school days and later as a youth leader, Bert encouraged young men to enjoy outdoor adventurous pursuits.

He soon realized that hiking and camping were valuable outlets for young men's energetic spirits. This aspect of his leadership led him to climb Ben Nevis in 1932. Over the following years he led 107 ascents to the summit of Ben Nevis.

Bert arranged for a group of young men to ascend Ben Nevis in the late summer of 1945. After an adventurous journey through a ferocious thunderstorm, missed rail connections and being given a lift on a goods train, the exhausted party of 33 boys and Bert settled down in a church hall close to the foot of Ben Nevis. Suddenly Bert woke the exhausted and sleepy lads by saying in a loud voice, "Lads, peace has been declared in Japan. We shall climb Ben Nevis this morning." It was Wednesday 15th August 1945 - V. J. Day.

Bert wanted to mark the day by thanking God for the peace that had been declared. Bert led the 'pilgrimage' of young men through the mist that swirled around Ben Nevis. With constant encouraging words from Bert, "We are nearly there", "Just over the top", "Just around the corner", the party, somewhat reluctantly, climbed with him to the summit. Once on the top, Bert, looking at the elated but exhausted lads, said that they should mark this very special day by building a 'peace cairn' to remember V. J. Day and those who had lost their lives.

One by one, the young men along with Bert gathered stones from the mountain and quickly a modest but significant cairn was built. When the last stone was put on the cairn, Bert Bissell led the young men in prayer to remember the war dead and prayed for world peace. He then blessed what was to become an internationally recognized Memorial Peace Cairn.

In 1949, a memorial plaque was fixed to the peace cairn which read:

TO THE GLORY OF GOD AND IN MEMORY OF THE FALLEN THIS CAIRN WAS ERECTED ON V.J. DAY AUG 15 1945 BY MEMBERS OF THE VICAR STREET METHODIST YOUNG MENS CLASS DUDLEY WORCS

Other plaques have since been added.

In 2003, the peace cairn was moved from its exposed position and re-erected close to the ruins of the old observatory (1883-1904). In 2006, there was a controversial proposal to remove the peace cairn from Ben Nevis' summit to the valley of Glen Nevis at the foot of the mountain. It was suggested that it could be placed near to where Bert was buried in Glen Nevis Cemetery and it would make the peace cairn more accessible to people without the need to climb the mountain. There was a move to clear the summit of the 50 or more 'miscellaneous mountain tributes' and to restore the remote atmosphere to the top of Ben Nevis. There was not only national dismay but an international outcry when the news got out that the peace cairn was to be taken off the mountain summit. Because of the international outrage, the plan to remove it from the mountain was shelved. Today, 'The Peace Cairn' remains the highest memorial in the United Kingdom.

From the earliest days following the end of WW2, Bert had a vision of a campaign for a prayerful and practical peace. Others caught the vision and joined him in campaigning for world peace. His campaigning for peace opened doors of welcome for Bert at the American, Japanese and Russian embassies in London.

Bert and the Vicar Street YMBC asked the Americans and Russians to broadcast messages of peace and goodwill from outer space. The Americans responded by making a call for peace from space when Frank Borman from Apollo 8, on Christmas Day 1968, said, "Give us, O God, the vision which can see Your love in the world in spite of human failure. Give us the faith to trust Your goodness in spite of our ignorance and weakness. Give us the knowledge that we may continue to pray with understanding hearts. And show us what each one of us can do to set forward the coming of the day of universal peace."

Bert Bissell's friendship towards the Japanese caused some people to be very critical of him for taking this stance. Some of his critics had suffered the atrocities meted out by the Japanese. Others had had relatives who had suffered at the hands of the Japanese. Nevertheless the Bible class formed an enduring friendly relationship with the atomic bomb destroyed city of Hiroshima.

This example of friendship inspired Dudley, Coventry Cathedral and Fort William to do the same. In 1962 the YMBC felt God inspiring them to invite the Japanese people to place a tablet on the Ben Nevis Peace Cairn. Some six years later, after many letters and visits to the Japanese embassy, a black granite plaque arrived from Hiroshima. It was carried up the mountain by a team of students from Nottingham and Sheffield universities and cemented on the peace cairn. Fort William and Dudley responded by sending to Hiroshima stone quarried from Ben Nevis. These stones form part of a peace cairn in the Peace Memorial Park in Hiroshima. The plaque reads in Japanese and English:

THE YOUTH OF FORT WILLIAM, SCOTLAND AND
DUDLEY, WORCESTERSHIRE, ENGLAND WHO

HAVE THEMSELVES BEEN LINKED IN FRIENDSHIP FOR MANY YEARS, HAVE PRESENTED THIS STONE TO THE YOUTH OF HIROSHIMA AS A SYMBOL OF GOODWILL AND DESIRE FOR RECONCILIATION AND WORLD PEACE 1972. THIS PARTICULAR STONE WAS HEWN FROM BRITAIN'S HIGHEST MOUNTAIN, BEN NEVIS, FORT WILLIAM, SCOTLAND

Bert also led peace climbs in the Republic of Ireland and Northern Ireland. In 1992, he went to South Africa as a roving peace ambassador, speaking at a rally by Table Mountain. Bert's campaigning for peace was recognised by many awards. Dudley Metropolitan Borough made him a Freeman in 1981. In 1987, he received the World Methodist Peace Award. Lochaber with its 'capital' town of the Highlands - Fort William - made him a Freeman. The Fort William Rotary Club presented him with 'The World Rotary International Medal'. After Bert died, a memorial was erected in the Dudley Coronation Gardens in his memory.

Bert died on the 2nd November 1998, aged 96, at Netherton, after fracturing his pelvis in a fall at his home in Selborne Road, Dudley. Vicar Street Methodist Church was full to overflowing for his funeral on 10th November and at his own request he was buried in the churchyard at the foot of Ben Nevis.

In his home was a copy of the famous painting in Dudley Art Gallery' 'Primitive Methodists at Prayer', by William Holt Yates Titcomb (1858-1930). The picture that inspired Bert over many years is a fitting reminder of the 20th century saintly man, Bertie

Bissell, who died on All Souls Day and whose funeral was on the eve on the annual solemn 'Remembrance of Armistice Day'.

Bert was a man of God, a man of prayer and spirituality, a Methodist local preacher for over 60 years, founder and leader of the Vicar Street Young Men's Bible Class, Lay pastor, a compassionate evangelist, peace campaigner, an outstandingly sensitive and caring probation officer. He was a man of the people who is remembered affectionately by countless thousands whose lives he enriched with his loving care. He was 'a Beacon of the 20th century' who brought the ray of light of the loving Christ to his own generation and whose faith blesses us with the reality of the everlasting peace of God.

Donald H. Ryan

THE SONS OF REV. FRANKLYN GEORGE SMITH

In Northgate Methodist Church, Warwick, [formerly Warwick Wesleyan Methodist Church] hangs a handwritten Roll of Honour commemorating 45 men and 3 women connected with the church who served in the Second World War. 5 men are shown as having been 'Killed in Action'. Surprisingly there is no similar Roll of Honour for the First World War. No one connected with the church has any recollection of seeing such a memorial. On a recent visit to the Warwickshire County Record Office, I came across a large volume in the Reference Library entitled *The County of Warwickshire Roll of Honour 1914-2005 – Volume 1 – South Warwickshire*, compiled by Keith Fowler and published by Able Publishing in 2005. Among the memorials shown to exist in Warwick was a Wesleyan Roll of Honour listing 36 men who had served in WW1. Apart from 2 men who had 'KinA' [Killed in Action] against their names, there was no indication whether the other 34 men had survived or had fallen in battle.

KINETON METHODIST CHURCH

At the same time as I made my initial discovery, I looked to see if the author had come across any further Methodist Rolls of Honour in South Warwickshire. I remembered seeing a Roll of

Honour in Kineton Methodist Church when attending a circuit meeting there in 2014. Yes, Kineton Wesleyan Methodist Church Roll of Honour was listed in Keith Fowler's book and to my surprise when I read through the list of names, I discovered that 2 sons of the Wesleyan Methodist minister at Kineton, Rev. Franklyn George Smith, were included. Both had been awarded the Military Cross for conspicuous gallantry and both later had been 'Killed in Action'.

Forgetting for a time my research connected with the Northgate Roll of Honour, I started looking into the history of the Smith family.

Franklyn George Smith was minister at Kineton from 1916-1919 according to my copy of *Hill's Arrangements* [1947 edition]. Earlier he had served in Spain for 32 years. After Kineton, he served in Priory Place, Doncaster, [1919-1922], Beverley, [1922-1925] and Marazion [1925-1929] before 'sitting down' in 1929. He retired to Maidstone, the town where he was born, but moved to Crowborough in Sussex in 1949 to live with his daughter, Eugenie, where he continued to be an active supernumerary until shortly before his death in March 1955.

Franklyn George Smith was born in Maidstone, Kent in 1859. He was the third son of Thomas Smith, glass and china dealer, accountant and Wesleyan local preacher. According to the *Who's Who of Methodism* [1933], he was educated at Maidstone Grammar School, before working in the family business and going on to Richmond College in Surrey to train for the Wesleyan Methodist Ministry. He was sent to Spain in 1884 and was to serve there for 32 years. He married Marie Laurence Empaytaz of Sonville, Switzerland. According to *Hill's Arrangements*, he had 4 sons, but his great nephew, Peter Ashley

Smith, who still lives in Kineton, states that he had 7 children – 4 sons and 3 daughters (another child died in infancy): Eugenie Marianne Augusta, born in Spain in 1889; Dora, born in 1891; Roderic Franklyn, born in Mahon, Minorca in 1893; Douglas George, born in Palma, Majorca in 1897; Maia 'Maisie' [year of birth not known]'; Gerald Eustace Franklyn, born in 1904 and Sydney Laurence, born in Barcelona in 1907.

Franklyn's obituary in the *Minutes of Conference* [1955] says, "He was the only official representative of the Methodist Church in Spain for 30 years during which his evangelical witness aroused much opposition and on more than one occasion his life was threatened. It was due to his efforts that a vigorous Christian Endeavour Movement was started. He translated a number of religious books for children of the schools, served on the Committee for the revision of the Spanish New Testament and compiled a Spanish-Greek Lexicon."

FRANKLYN GEORGE SMITH'S FAMOUS SONS

Roderic Franklyn Smith was born in Mahon, Minorca according to the 1911 Census of Grantham, Lincolnshire. At the time of the census he was a 19-year-old mechanical engineering pupil at an ironworks, lodging with Miss Martha Elizabeth Cooper, a boarding house keeper, at 154 Harrowby Road, Grantham, only a short distance from Finkin Street Wesleyan Methodist Chapel where a few years later Margaret Hilda Roberts [later Thatcher] and her family worshipped.

According to Gillian Ashley-Smith in *Kineton in the Great War* [Brewin Books, 1998], Roderic enlisted in the Seaforth Highlanders as a private and after 10 months in France he was commissioned in the King's Shropshire Light Infantry for distinguished conduct in the attack on Langemark in August 1917. In November 1917, in the advance on Cambrai, he was awarded the Military Cross and later a bar. In the London Gazette of February 1918, the following citation was published:

> During an attack it was found that Tanks leading companies of the battalion veered off and were hotly engaged. Although the trenches had not been fully cleared of the enemy, he volunteered in spite of heavy fire, to find both companies and tanks and succeeded in leading them back, with the result of the complete capture of the objective assigned to the battalion. To this success his courage and initiative greatly contributed.

In March 1918, by which time he had been promoted to Captain, the Germans launched a major offensive against the 60th Brigade. Sadly, on 28th March he was killed in action and, due to the intensity of the battle, he was buried in an unmarked grave. His name is inscribed on the Pozieres Memorial.

Douglas George Smith was born in 1897 in Palma, Majorca according to the 1911 Census. At that time he was a 14-year-old pupil at the famous Methodist Boarding School for Children of Methodist Ministers – Kingswood School in Bath. After leaving Kingswood School, he entered St Catherine's College, Cambridge to read Modern Languages, but as soon as he reached military age he enlisted in September 1915. After completing his initial training, he was commissioned in the 6th [Service] Battalion, King's Shropshire Light Infantry, arriving in France on Saturday 25th December 1915. He was awarded the Military Cross in June 1916. His citation in the London Gazette, 27th July

1916, states that it was for conspicuous gallantry on patrol when he crawled up to an enemy parapet and listened for 2 hours whilst wounded before returning to his lines. The information he learned proved to be of considerable importance. Twice wounded in action, he returned to the trenches in February 1917 after several months' recuperation [at Kineton?] and was promoted to Second Lieutenant on his 21st birthday. Sadly he died shortly afterwards on Thursday 16th August 1917 having been severely wounded in action and was buried in Dozinghem Military Cemetery in Belgium.

His entry in Warwickshire Roll of Honour – 1914-2005 on page 117 reads:

> **SMITH – Douglas George**, [Military Cross] – 104707, Lieutenant 6th [Service] Battalion, King's Shropshire Light infantry, 60th Brigade, 20th Light Division. Died of abdomen wounds in No 47 Casualty Clearing Station on Thursday 16th August 1917, aged 21. Second son of Rev. Franklyn George Smith and Marie L Smith of 10 Town Moor Avenue, Doncaster. He was born in Palma, Majorca, educated at St Catherine's College, Cambridge. Enlisted September 1915 and arrived in France on Saturday 25th December 1915. Awarded Military Cross [London Gazette, Thursday 27th July, 1916] – "For conspicuous gallantry on patrol. He went right up to the enemy's parapet, and though wounded, remained out for 2 hours to verify what he heard. He has shown great coolness and bravery on many occasions." His father was Wesleyan Minister in Kineton from 1916. Buried in Dozinghem Military Cemetery, Poperinge, West-Vlaanderen, Belgium. He is commemorated on the Wesleyan Methodist Church Memorial with his brother Roderic Franklyn Smith.

What brave men! I have only scratched the surface to write this short article. I am indebted to Peter Ashley Smith for supplying me with several pages of his research into the lives of his 2 great uncles and to Peter's wife, Gillian, for permission to quote extracts from her book *Kineton in The Great War* [page 82]. Sue Tall, of Kenilworth Methodist Church, an expert in the history of war memorials, also provided valuable information on Rev. Franklyn Smith's time in Spain by locating an online reprint of *The History of The Wesleyan Methodist Missionary Society, Volume 4* by G. G. Findlay, 1921 [pages 430-431], reprinted in 2013 by Forgotten Books, London.

Now I must get back to work on my original piece of research - discovering more about the men whose names are on the Roll of Honour for WW1, for Warwick Wesleyan Methodist Church.

Richard Ratcliffe

METHODIST MILLION

From The Birmingham Daily Argus, *26*[th] *July 1898*

"The Wesleyan Conference [at Hull] was crowded yesterday when Mr R W Perks, M.P., proposed to inaugurate the scheme for collecting a million guineas from a million adherents. He would like to see £200,000 devoted to educational purposes, some of it to fight the cause of Methodist children in the country parishes where the population was largely Nonconformist but where the schools were in the hands of bigoted clergymen, a Central Hall in London which might be bought at a cost of £250,000 to seat 3,000 people and have attached to it all the offices and rooms needed by the Methodist departments. Dr Stephenson's Home might receive £50,000 to help the effort now being made to prevent a single Methodist child from being brought up in a pauper school. The raising of the money he thought could be done by inscribing every Wesleyan name on a 'Church Roll' and those who could afford to give more than a guinea could subscribe the surplus at the rate of a guinea in the name of a poor person on the Roll."

Rev. W L Watkinson, ex-President of the Conference, seconded the proposal to raise the million. The Conference at once passed it and referred it to a committee to decide upon the methods of procedure.

The Million Guinea Fund or Twentieth Century Fund was officially opened on 1st January 1899 and closed on 1st January 1901, when a list of donors in every church or circuit was read out at services held on that day and these lists preserved in a Historic Roll with the historical documents of the Wesleyan Methodist Church.

The Historic Roll would include the names of all donors and collectors, whether members of the Wesleyan Methodist Church, teachers or scholars in Sunday and day schools, communicants, seat holders or other worshippers, or adherents and friends of Methodism at home and abroad. In no case would the amounts given or collected be recorded in the Historic Roll.

When the Executive Committee met on 5th December 1900, the fund stood at £423,696 so it was agreed to extended the closing. This was done twice more until it was agreed to wind up the Twentieth Century Fund at the 1904 Conference in Sheffield when it stood at £1,007,229. After allowing more time for all the circuits to return their portions of the Historic Roll, the Executive Committee agreed on 23rd June 1908 to bind the Roll even though 13 circuits out of 831 still had not returned their lists of donors. By this time the fund stood at £1,073,682.

A special bookcase was commissioned to be placed in the New Hall [Westminster Central Hall] where the Historic Roll would be stored and exhibited. When Westminster Central Hall was opened on 3rd October 1912, the Historic Roll had been bound into 50 large volumes comprising more than 17,000 pages and containing the names of over 1,025,000 donors. The bookcase containing the 50 volumes can be seen in the Visitors' Centre to the right of the reception desk.

At the time of the collection, the West Midlands area was a huge District – The Birmingham and Shrewsbury District. The district was made up of 48 circuits plus Handsworth Wesleyan Ministers' Training College. The number of donors and names of people for whom a donation was given 'In Memoriam' was 22,419.

To qualify to sign the Historic Roll a person had to give or collect a guinea or more. A person could give a guinea or more on behalf of another person or in memory of a loved one or family member who had died. Any person who after bona fide efforts to give a guinea could not, in the judgement of the Circuit Committee, be reasonably expected to comply with the above conditions. Any child or Sunday school scholar who had donated a shilling or more was also permitted to sign the Historic Roll.

Every adult donor received a signed certificate printed on a card measuring 14 inches by 11 inches as their official receipt, whilst each child received a John Wesley medallion.

The Twentieth Century Fund Treasurers' Account Book shows that the Children's Collection raised £4,162 0s 1d and that 90,000 medallions were struck.

Both the certificates and the medallions are now collectors' items. Have you got one or both in your family archive?

Volume 21 comprises 20 circuits in Birmingham, West Bromwich, Walsall and Wolverhampton, while Volume 22 is made up of 28 circuits in Warwickshire, Worcestershire, Leicestershire, Staffordshire, Salop and Herefordshire.

Volume 21 Circuits and donors are as follows:-
Birmingham
Moseley Road Circuit – 701 donors gave £1500 3s 2d.
Central Mission Circuit – 762 donors - £1252 12s 8d.
North Mission Circuit – 366 donors - £388 10s 0d
Nechells Circuit – list of donors is missing but the Twentieth Century Fund Treasurers' Account Book shows that the Circuit donated £140 14s 0d.
Belmont Row Circuit – 563 donors - £985 6s 4d.
Aston Park Circuit – 376 donors -£680 13s 0d.
Sutton Park Circuit – 183 donors - £1155 0s 0d.
Wesley Circuit – 1301 donors - £4292 2s 5d.
Handsworth College – 64 donors - £345 9s 0d.
Welsh Circuit – 15 donors - £10 0s 0d.
Islington Circuit – 50 donors - £3680 15s 8d.
Bristol Road Circuit – 467 donors - £861 1s 4d.
Smethwick Circuit – 626 donors - £794 0s 0d.

West Bromwich
Wesley Circuit – 989 donors - £1575 0s 0d.
Hill Top Circuit – 819 donors - £1942 10s 0d.

Wednesbury
Wednesbury Circuit – 1602 donors - £1575 0s 0d.

Walsall
Wesley Circuit – 642 donors - £1050 0s 0d.

Centenary Circuit – 756 donors - £701 4s 0d.

Willenhall
Willenhall Circuit – 417 donors - £631 6s 6d.

Wolverhampton
Darlington Street – 1148 donors - £1493 2s 4d.
Trinity Circuit – 519 donors - £2306 0s 0d.
Total number of donors' names – 12,366. Amount donated - £27,360 10s 5d.

Volume 22 circuits and donors are as follows:-
Bilston Circuit – 795 donors gave £1474 13s 0d.
Dudley Circuit – 779 donors - £867 17s 6d.
Tipton Circuit – 361 donors - £414 18s 1d.
Oldbury Circuit – 165 donors - £317 8s 8d.
Stourbridge Circuit – 820 donors - £1057 5s 10d.
Cradley Circuit – 224 donors - £280 5s 0d.
Stourport Circuit – 191 donors - £232 16s 0d.
Kidderminster Circuit – 257 donors - £302 19s 5d.
Worcester Circuit – 323 donors - £378 0s 0d.
Malvern Mission Circuit – 138 donors - £168 5s 0d.
Bromsgrove Circuit – 170 donors - £444 11s 3d.
Evesham Circuit – 193 donors - £247 3s 6d.
Redditch Circuit – 465 donors - £649 13s 3d.
Coventry Circuit – 446 donors - £482 16s 3d.
Rugby Circuit – 593 donors - £650 10s0d.
Leamington Circuit – 722 donors - £1011 11s 5d.
Stratford upon Avon Circuit – 160 donors - £195 2s 6d.
Hinckley Circuit – 601 donors - £630 0s 0d.

Nuneaton & Atherstone Circuit – 423 donors - £1577 9s 9d.
Shrewsbury Circuit – 455 donors - £784 16s 10d.
Madeley Circuit – 249 donors - £264 7s 5d.
Dawley Circuit – 196 donors - £242 11s 0d.
Wellington [Salop] Circuit – 397 donors - £616 12s 6d.
Ketley Bank & Shifnal Circuit – 158 donors - £185 9s 0d.
Ludlow Circuit – 276 donors - £317 15s 6d.
Kington Circuit – 125 donors - £173 5s 0d.
Leominster Circuit – 213 donors - £284 0s 9d.
Knighton Circuit – 158 donors - £166 1s 10d.

Total number of donors' names – 10053. Amount donated - £14416 16s 3d.

WESLEY DEACONESS CONVOCATION, BIRMINGHAM, JUNE 1ST-7TH 1923

General Instructions (adapted from Agenda 1923*)*

We are to meet this year without Mr Bradfield [Rev. William Bradfield] (died 4th January 1923), and it is a sore loss . . . Everyone will be glad to know that Mrs Bradfield will be with us . . . We owe a great deal to our friends at Birmingham; to the Rev. Frederick H. Benson for his sympathy and help, to the Rev. Percy J. Grubb and the Rev. Ernest Nicholas, the local secretaries who have taken no end of trouble for us, and to the hosts and hostesses who are giving us hospitality. Perhaps by the grace of God we may in turn leave behind us some good thing.

Convocation opens at the Central Hall on Friday evening, when there will be a reception at 7.00pm by Councillor and Mrs Terry, of Redditch, to which our hosts and hostesses are invited. The Central Hall is about ten minutes' walk from the railway station. Sisters may assemble there any time from about 6 o'clock onwards. Readers will observe that the morning addresses, from 9.45am to 10.45am, will be free to Sisters and any friends who may care to come. The evening meetings are, of course, public.

Sisters, who are attending Convocation, will receive with this *Agenda*, a copy of the Convocation Roll and an envelope for travelling expenses. Please bring these with you to Convocation. The travelling expenses envelope should be marked with the amount of the railway fare and handed in at Reception. A voucher for the reduced railway fare is also enclosed. We shall be pleased to supply vouchers to any friends who are attending Convocation.

Sisters attending will number about 235. 38 deaconesses had asked for leave of absence. They were mainly retired, elderly or sick. 25 deaconesses could not attend because they were serving abroad.

Programme (Brief Details)

Friday, June 1. Central Hall, Corporation Street
   7.00pm. Reception by Mr Charles Terry, J.P. C.C. and Mrs Terry
   Welcome Address – Rev. Dr J. G. Tasker (Handsworth College)

Saturday, June 2.
Open session – morning prayers; lecture 'Our Gospel' (i) - Rev. W. Russell Maltby
Business session – Convocation Record; official questions; committee nominations; notices of motion; the work of the Order (i)
Afternoon – visit to Kingsmead College, Selly Oak

Sunday, June 3
11.00am. Convocation sermon – Rev. W. Russell Maltby (Warden)
6.30pm. Services in various churches conducted by Warden, Rev. Colin A. Roberts and deaconesses

Monday June 4
Open session – morning prayers; lecture 'Our Gospel' (ii) - Rev. W. Russell Maltby
Business session – Ceylon Mission Fund; election of representatives to committee; notices of motion; the work of the Order (ii)
7.30pm. Public Consecration Service – at Moseley Road conducted by the President of Conference, the Rev. John E. Wakerley
8 probationer deaconesses to be 'fully received' into the Order

Tuesday, June 5
Open session – morning prayers; lecture – 'Evangelism' – Rev. Colin A. Roberts
Business session; the work of the Order (iii); Annual meeting of the Wesley Deaconesses' Annuitant Friendly Society; Annual meeting of the Deaconess Tent of the Independent Order of Rechabites. Chairman: Mrs Bradfield
3.00pm. Visit to Bournville by invitation of Messrs Cadbury Bros.
7.30pm. Public Foreign Missionary meeting at Islington

Speakers were 4 missionary deaconesses, the Rev. William C. Bird (Ceylon) (he married Wesley Deaconess Annie Capper in 1909) and the Warden

Wednesday, June 6
Open session – morning prayers; lecture – 'Evangelism' - Rev. Colin A. Roberts
Business session - the work of the Order (iv)
7.30pm. Public Anniversary meeting - The Central Hall
Chairman: G. Davis Green, Esq. (Wolverhampton). Speakers included Mrs Stuart Moore (Evelyn Underhill), a deaconess and 3 ministers.

Thursday, June 7
10.00am Holy Communion.

WESLEY DEACONESS ORDER CONVOCATIONS 1933/4

CONVOCATION 1933, SHEFFIELD

In April 1933, the first United Convocation of the Deaconess Order was held in Sheffield. On Thursday 5th April at 11.15am, the Wesley, the United Methodist and the Primitive Methodist Sisters met in separate sessions. Matters relating to the unified Order were discussed such as the uniform and the name of the Order.

Uniform

The Uniform Committee recommended that the following be the recognised uniform of the Order. (1) Headdress. A bonnet with navy veil, three fine grey stripes round the crown and down the centre of the veil, with the alternative of a plain felt hat bearing the recognised hat band of grey-bordered navy and woven badge. (2) Dress. A plain navy dress, white collars and cuffs, white tie if bonnet is worn or navy tie with hat. In the case of probationers the dress was to be grey. (3) Coat. This was to be plain navy. (4) Other details were to be left to the good taste of the individual.

Name Of The Order

After much discussion by all the groups, separately and together, it was felt that a 'denominational' label should be avoided and it was queried as to whether the term 'Wesley' was not regarded by outsiders as denominational. It was felt that the word 'Methodist' should somehow be included. Sister Mary Hunter (Tutor) urged Convocation to take the long view, reminding us that in a few years 'Wesleyanism' will be a thing of the past and the sectional labels will be forgotten. Mr Thorn (Rev. George W. Thorn, Joint Secretary) then suggested that 'Wesley Deaconess Order of the Methodist Church' should be forwarded as a recommendation of the Convocation to Conference. The final resolution was moved, seconded by deaconesses from all three sections and carried unanimously. It read as follows:

"This Convention expresses its judgement that it is desirable that the custom of calling such an Order by the name of some revered personality in the history of the Church should be followed. And seeing that the Methodism in all its branches traces its origin and inspiration to the life and labours of John Wesley and that the name 'Wesley' cannot be regarded as sectional or as belonging to our old divisions, but rather as symbolising our common heritage, the Convocation recommends to the Committee that the Order now united be called 'The Wesley Deaconess Order of the Methodist Church'.'

CONVOCATION 1934, BIRMINGHAM

The 1934 Convocation was held in the Central Hall, Birmingham (13-19th April). Miss Millicent Brownhill, Superintendent of the Shaftesbury House Girls' Hostel, connected with the Birmingham Mission, acted as hostess, deputising for Mrs W. Cadbury who was indisposed. She conveyed Mrs Cadbury's best wishes 'for a helpful and inspirational Convocation'. The Rev. Frederick H. Benson, Chairman of the District, and the Rev., E. Benson Perkins, Superintendent of the Mission, welcomed the members of the Order.

On Saturday the 14th, there was a special reception meeting for the receiving ex-Primitive Methodist Sisters into the Order. The Rev. Dr. W. Russell Maltby, Warden of the Order, read the add receiving resolution, which had been forwarded from the committee:

"We wish to welcome into the fellowship of the Wesley Deaconess Order of the Methodist Church all the ex-Primitive Methodist Sisters who desire such admission and are approved by the recognised authority of the ex-PM Church."

Then the Rev. George E. Wiles (Primitive Methodist) gave the names of the eleven ex-Primitive Methodist Sisters present and said a little about their work. They went forward to be welcomed by Dr Maltby and Sister Ruth Northcroft (retiring

Vice President of the Order) and were then presented with the badge of the Deaconess Order by the Rev. Robert W. Gair (the ex-United Methodist Warden who was now joint secretary of the unified Order). Another eleven Sisters who were not present were named also. A further Primitive Methodist Sister came to Convocation later in the week, making a total of twenty-three who joined the unified Order.

Three Methodist Missionary Society students who had spent the year studying at the Wesley Deaconess College, Ilkley, prior to going overseas, were welcomed into the fellowship of the Order, though at this stage they were not entering the Order. After these two special events, Convocation followed its usual pattern of conversation on the work of God. In the afternoon, most of the deaconesses went on a coach trip, provided generously by Mr A. M. Patrick (of Patrick Motors, a well known firm) to Stratford-upon-Avon where they visited the new Shakespeare Memorial Theatre (opened 1932) as well as 'other places of interest' before returning to Birmingham via Warwick and Kenilworth.

The morning service on Sunday was held in the Central Hall, the sermon being preached by Rev. Dr W. Russell Maltby, while the deaconesses took preaching services in Birmingham in the afternoon and evening. Monday saw the business meeting taking place with the usual questions being asked and answered. These included listing those who were present, including a welcome to three deaconesses on furlough from West Africa (Evelyn Bellamy, Frances Green, and Edith Spears), those absent and why and greetings from Sisters serving overseas. There was the naming of the eleven received on probation, the seven who had retired, one who was 'resting', and the five who had resigned because they had married. It was noted that no one had died during the year and that ten Sisters had served for twenty-one years. Reports were given, appointments made and a notice of motion about the possibility of having a magazine or extended newsletter published. In the afternoon, a group of the deaconesses visited the Selly Oak Colleges and were entertained to tea at the George Cadbury Hall by Mr and Mrs Edward Cadbury. The evening Missionary meeting was held in the Acocks Green Church, with addresses given by overseas Sisters plus short contributions from four who were about to go out to the mission field. Following the early morning worship three of the students presented *The Mess of Pottage*, one of the plays of St Francis. Then the three sections of the Order separated for their own sessions, in order to discuss any outstanding business connected with their original Orders and to facilitate the smooth integration into one body. Having come back together the deaconesses assembled in the Large Hall for a group photograph.

The 1934 Consecration Service was held in the Moseley Road Church, conducted by the President of Conference, the Rev. F. Luke Wiseman, when seven deaconesses were received into the Order.

Worship on the Wednesday morning was led by the President of Conference, who not only gave an address on 'Cornelius', but taught Convocation a new hymn tune – unfortunately the records do not give details of either! Then the various sections gave reports of their individual sessions and discussion followed on several points.

Mr Gair explained how Methodist Union had affected the ex-UM appointments so that there were some deaconesses currently without appointments. Dr Maltby replied that he would be only too glad for all the appointments to be merged as soon as possible.

Sister Phyllis Shafto reported on the Ceylon Fund, which had been set up in 1903 by the Wesley Deaconesses to support their Sisters serving in Ceylon and she announced the date of the College Missionary Anniversary.

Then there was an extended and lively discussion on the report of the Committee on Women in the Ministry, which had been presented to the 1933 Methodist Conference. The recommendations of the Committee were to be sent down to the May Synods and, if approved, they would be ratified by the coming Conference. Finally, the following resolution was put and passed unanimously:

"That the Wesley Deaconess Order appreciates the proposals now before the Methodist Church, and hopes that such difficulties as still remain may be successfully surmounted, so that the door may be opened as early as possible for such women as God has called to enter into the itinerant ministry." [*Details of the discussion below.]

Before the evening public meeting, the deaconess' choir sang a selection of hymns from the new hymn book (MHB, 1932). In the public meeting, chaired by Miss Lorna Shirley-Smith, Sister Elizabeth Trethewey (East London Mission) sang two solos and Sisters Rhoda Marchant (Hoxton) and Mary McCord (Dagenham) gave graphic accounts of their work.

The closing session on Thursday 19th April saw any final items of business being concluded and thanks expressed to Birmingham friends who had provided hospitality and to all those who had made the local arrangements.

*Women In The Ministry Convocation Discussion

Dr Maltby said, that although he thought the idea of uniting the existing ministries of women and forming a new Order of Women's Ministry was very good in its way, he did not want to see women's work more segregated than at present, nor the difference between men's and women's ministry work accentuated.

Sister Nellie Atkins spoke of the long probation a woman candidate would have to pass through before she was a fully ordained minister if she had to enter the ministry first through the doors of the W.D.O.; three or four years in the deaconess work and then the usual seven years. The Warden thought the first part of the training might be considered sufficient to lessen the second part, but he thought it certainly would be eight or nine years. He said that that might not be a bad thing at first and he wished there were such a test for men. Mr Thorn thought such facilities as were now offered for entering the Ministry should be accepted and that later on the door would no doubt be wider. Sisters took part in the discussion, stress being laid on the importance of pastoral work in the ministry, and whether the itinerant ministry offered more scope for a woman than the present Deaconess Order. The Warden said it was not a question merely of status and illustrated 'how the work of the Deaconesses was limited' [at the moment].

E Dorothy Graham

Sources: Record of Convocation (1892-1935), *Minutes of Convocation (1892-1969);* The Agenda (*WDO Magazine*) 1933 & 1934

ARCHIVES AND HERITAGE

Reflections from Thomas Skinner (1913-2002)

Fifty years ago, there was no such thing as formal Methodist or Wesley archives. Bearing in mind that the Methodist Church had then existed for over 200 years, it seems to me a little strange that our forefathers were so slow in setting up what is a most essential part of our church heritage.

Those of you who are my age and older will remember the divisions prior to Union on 20th September 1932. As a youth of 19, I remember that day well, the President telling us that we were now one Church. (The Methodist Church of Great Britain was created in 1932 by the union of the Wesleyan Methodist Church 1744-1932, Primitive Methodist Church 1810-1932, and the United Methodist Church 1907-1932. The United Methodist Church was formed in 1907 when the Methodist New Connexion 1797-1907, Bible Christians 1815-1907, and the United Methodist Free Churches 1857-1907 amalgamated.)

It was in the 1950s that Rev. Dr Frank Baker and Rev. Dr John C. Bowmer told the Conference that records should be kept, but it was not until 1973 that Conference finally acted. I had just retired for the first time when one morning I walked into the Office at Lyndon to find Rev. Stanley K. Chesworth sitting in the chair. "Thomas," he said, "you love Methodist history, don't you? Would you like to be our Methodist

Archivist?" "Yes," I replied. "I will have to see the Super (Superintendent) and the Circuit will have to agree," he said.

In due course, I was elected as Elmdon Circuit Archivist. The Super, Rev. Thomas L. Thexton, came to me on Saturday 27th July 1974, with seven bundles of books and papers. He was due to retire on the following Monday.

He caught me totally unawares and even if I know someone from Church or Circuit is coming (my wife, Millie, will tell you) I get into a bit of a tizz. I had started work again, so only had Saturdays to attend to the records. Firstly, I had to repair some of them, then label them, record them in a formal ledger and then make lists for the Church Secretary to type for me. I never handed over my records to the library without proper documentation – my Civil Service upbringing had taught me this. Initially, Mr David Eades of Halesowen (Birmingham District Archivist) would come and collect the completed batches and deposit them in the library, then when he resigned, I began taking them to the Reference Library to deposit them myself.

The collecting of new items has not always proved an easy task and some church people prefer to keep memorabilia for themselves. One lady, who shall remain nameless, said to me, "Don't come bothering me, I live for today and not in the past!" May I make one plea to stewards and secretaries not to hang on to old minute books at home or in your church cupboards. Seek out old baptismal, marriage records, cash books, class lists etc. and hand them over to the Superintendent Minister when he visits your church and he will pass them onto me.

These are the activities I undertake:

- Collate, categorise and register them in an Acquisitions Ledger.

- Repair books, papers, pamphlets,
- Compile lists for typing; take records to Reference Library with typed lists.

Memoirs of Thomas Skinner, Elmdon Circuit Archivist and Wesley Historical Society - West Midlands Branch Archivist until his death in 2002.
Passed on by his family

Methodism has come a long way since 1973. The Church and its officers continue to strive to raise awareness of the importance of archiving our records, not because we desire to look backwards with nostalgia to the time when our Sunday schools and churches were full to overflowing, but because we seek to preserve our heritage for future generations. We continue to tell our church's story and to celebrate where we have come from, to affirm our journey today and to be inspired for the future. We had some wonderful examples and illustrations at the 2015 Methodist Conference of ways in which we can use our history and heritage to tell our story and reach out to today's generation.

The Methodist Church, its officers, archivists and historians highlight how our heritage can be used to shape our mission and outreach today. The world is a very different place to 50 years ago. The growth of computers, the internet and worldwide web, has helped encourage the growth of interest in genealogy and historical research and this is one way we can connect to the present day generation and reach out to people we wouldn't otherwise have contact with.

It remains important to continue to promote archiving of records and documents and I often encourage people to give me all their records as it is difficult to assess what is and isn't archival without looking at it. The golden rule for me is: "Does this item, record, photo, document, pamphlet help to tell the story of this church or circuit and will it make sense to people in the future?"

There are many challenges, not least what do we do with artefacts that come into our possession when churches close? How do we make the most of the missional opportunities we have, given the many Methodist chapels on Living History Museum sites? How do we best use our archives, history and heritage to reach out to people with the message of the Gospel in the present age?

Diane Webb